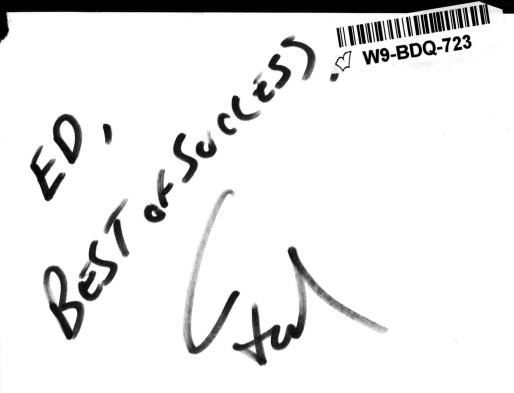

ED,
BEST of SUCCESS)

Praise for *Superpower!*

"Ford Saeks is a master. Period. This straight-talk, no-nonsense guide will shift your thought process and laser focus your results. The guy's a genius."

—**Shawne Duperon,**
CEO, ShawneTV

"Unleash your potential and your organization's potential by implementing the simple strategies in *Superpower!* that can be applied to all levels of your organization from the top down and from the bottom up!"

—**Les Brown,**
CEO, Les Brown Enterprises

"Time and time again, I find myself turning to Ford Saeks for advice and counsel. I have come to rely upon his straightforward communication style, common sense, and critical thinking to drive me toward better results for marketing our business."

—**Carrie Burrell,**
VP, Marketing Manager, Mission Valley Bank

"If you want to improve the quality of your life and the lives of those you care about, then read and implement the strategies that Ford reveals in *Superpower!*"

—**Michael Krisa,**
EasyWebVideo.com

"*Superpower!* is filled with straight talk and endless ideas to help improve your results in both business and everyday life."

—**Jeffrey Gitomer,**
CEO, Buy Gitomer, Inc.

"This book is what everyone needs today if they are going to succeed. The new economic realities dictate that we must change the mindsets from which we operate. If you want to be at the top of your game and enjoy life the way you want it to be, you need to read *Superpower!* You can bet your competition is reading it, too."

—**Ron Karr,**
author of *Lead, Sell or Get Out of the Way*

"Ford Saeks has achieved great success by working smart and working hard, and he shows you how to get things done faster and easier."

—**Brian Foster,**
CEO, United Sports Solutions, Inc.

"If you are looking for a road map to take your potential for success and turn it into a reality, then Ford's book is a must read!"

—**Steven A. Sims,**
CEO, Vertex Home Improvement

"Ford has overcome tough odds to achieve great success by working smart and working hard. This book shows you how he did it and how you can do it, too. He'll help you achieve superpower, not through magic or gimmicks, but by using his proven strategies and tactics. Read it if you want super results."

—**Mark Sanborn,**
speaker and best-selling author of *The Fred Factor* and *You Don't Need a Title to Be a Leader*

"Everybody has the ability to be extraordinary ... everybody. Ford Saeks has discovered how to unleash the overlooked power available to you. He's done it in his own amazing life and can show you how to do the same. Activate your Superpower before another minute of extraordinary living passes you by."

—**Jim Cathcart,**
author of *The Acorn Principle*

"Ford Saeks has the experience, insights, and unique perspective to show you how to become a Superpower. This book is a must read today, as tomorrow your competitors will have it!"

— **Sam Silverstein,**
founder, The Accountability Academy

"This book shows how to leap your financial position in life to the next level. Ford provides one 'aha' after another. I often ask myself, 'Wow—why didn't I think of that before? This is going to produce great results and is so much easier to do than the way I've done it all along!' Save yourself the effort of trying harder to produce the results you want. This book shows you the ways to make better choices—and that leads to financial success both in your personal life and in your work life!"

— **Michael Foster,**
CISA, CISSP, author of *The Secure CEO: How to Protect Your Computer Systems, Your Company, and Your Job*

"Ford Saeks is the one expert to listen to when you want to go from zero to 100 in the least amount of time with the least amount of effort."

— **Jack McDonough,**
CEO, BlackFin Licensing, LLC

"Ford inspires us to perform better than we ever thought we could. His ideas not only work, they help us generate great ideas of our own. Ford truly teaches how to approach the world from a different, more profitable angle."

— **Chad Hoffman,**
President and CEO, The Richwood Banking Company

"Ford is probably this county's brightest and most potent marketer in industry today. His insights to solving problems are brilliant and his ability to collaborate with others in providing amazing solutions is remarkable. Ford understands the subtle, yet important marketing nuences that will either make or break a company! That in itself is an art! His willingness to help others supports his "prosperity mindset" to make a better world for all he meets."

—Robert Smith,
President, Axcelerate worldwide

"When you read *Superpower!* you will become superpowerful. You'll learn how to stop stumbling along the same old road you've been on. Ford shows you the shorcut that leads to your success in work and in life. Follow his easy-to-understand priciples and you'll be where you want to be. Ford is a brilliant forward thinker whose path to success is captured in this book."

—Pam Lontos,
President of Pam Lontos Consulting

SUPERPOWER!

HOW TO **THINK, ACT,** AND **PERFORM** WITH **LESS EFFORT** AND **BETTER RESULTS**

FORD SAEKS

WILEY

John Wiley & Sons, Inc.

Published by John Wiley & Sons, Inc., Hoboken, New Jersey.
Published simultaneously in Canada

For general information on our other products and services or for technical support, please contact our Customer Care Department within the United States at (800) 762-2974, outside the United States at (317) 572-3993 or fax (317) 572-4002.

Wiley publishes in a variety of print and electronic formats and by print-on-demand. Some material included with standard print versions of this book may not be included in e-books or in print-on-demand. If this book refers to media such as a CD or DVD that is not included in the version you purchased, you may download this material at http://booksupport.wiley.com. For more information about Wiley products, visit www.wiley.com.

Library of Congress Cataloging-in-Publication Data:

Saeks, Ford, 1961–
  Superpower! : how to think, act, and perform with less effort and better results / Ford Saeks.
    p. cm.
  ISBN 978-1-118-27786-7 (cloth); ISBN 978-1-118-33063-0 (ebk); ISBN 978-1-118-33131-6 (ebk); ISBN 978-1-118-33347-1 (ebk)
  1. Success. 2. Success in business. 3. Self-actualization (Psychology) I. Title.
  BF637.S8.S236 2012
  650.1–dc23
                                                        2012009224

Printed in the United States of America.

10 9 8 7 6 5 4 3 2 1

Contents

THE SUPERPOWER JOURNEY

Superpower! takes you on a Superpower Journey, where you'll discover **seven steps** that will help you solve problems faster, make better decisions, and improve your professional and personal life. The steps of the journey, which you should take in order, are laid out here.

CONTENTS

CONTENTS

Read This

Most people skip the acknowledgments pages. I'm going to challenge you to read this one, because it explains why I wrote the book in the first place.

This book is a compilation of strategies, tactics, ideas, and concepts that I've used throughout my life on my journey of success and fulfillment. Some of these ideas may sound familiar, while others may sound outrageous. Every effort has been made to give credit to other authors or thought leaders for their contribution to my success in the strategies. You see, I've been on the road of personal growth and development for more than 40 years. I've read countless books, listened to countless audio programs, and attended hundreds of seminars on a wide variety of topics. Therefore, if any of these ideas sound familiar, it's because they must've been used and taught by other thought leaders. I have credited everyone I could possibly think of, and I spent a lot of time thinking about it, but anyone who reads this book should be aware that many of the ideas that appear here are just parts of my psyche. So let's look at that now.

As a business growth expert and professional speaker (you can read more about that at ProfitRichResults.com), I've presented to hundreds of thousands of people from organizations around the globe on a variety of business-related and success topics. Those topics include innovation, business growth, creativity, strategic planning, direct response marketing, Internet marketing, social media marketing, and success strategies.

As a consultant, I've worked with hundreds of companies of all sizes to help them find, attract, and keep their customers; increase the performance of their teams; and increase their sales and profits. That process always starts with evaluating where people and organizations are now, identifying where they want to go, and then developing the strategic plan and specific action steps to reach their goals. Working through this process over and over again, applying different strategies, and making adjustments and course corrections has given me unique insights into how people think and make decisions and whether they're going to take the action steps necessary to produce results that they want. Some may say that I'm really just a marketing expert, and I'm fine with that definition. Why? Because my definition of *marketing* is just giving people enough information that they can make good decisions. Marketing is just communication. And the purpose of communication is the response it elicits.

If you're a good marketer, what that means is that you're skilled at understanding buyer behaviors, identifying needs, and then creating and delivering unique value propositions that get people to take action to fulfill a need or desire. It's not manipulation or hype; it's communication. And that's what most of the principles in this book emerged from: my own communication (with myself and with others) about delivering value.

My goal for this book is to give you and the people you care about insights on using your superpower. My definition of superpower is simple: **the ability to use your mind to make decisions, develop your critical thinking skills, and produce the results you desire in your life.**

Now, I waited many years to write this book, because, honestly, I didn't feel worthy to tackle the topic of superpower. There are so many other books on the market that claim to have the answer to success and achievement, and some of them are excellent. I felt like it really wasn't necessary for me to write this book ... until now.

What changed? With the advances in technology and how people now consume information, I realized that the way people learn and the way they implement that learning had changed. It's because of these changes and what's going on in the world today that I felt now is the right time for this book.

Here's what I'm getting at. I've been an entrepreneur since I was 12 years old. I listened to my first motivational cassette program while I was in a detention center for troubled boys. It was those words of positive encouragement and new ideas that expanded my thinking and put me on the path to success. Over the years, I've founded and grown multiple companies, and I've been responsible for hundreds of employees. Over many years of life experience, I've sought out experts who've done what I wanted to do, so I could learn from them, model their behavior, and produce similar or even better results. To acknowledge every single person who helped me along the way would fill an entire shelf of books, even if I could remember all of their names, which I can't. So I'm going to do my best to recognize the most important collaborators, allies, and mentors here and throughout the book, and I'm going to apologize in advance for anybody I left out.

The first name on my list of people to thank belongs to my wife, Aliesa George. Aliesa has believed in me at those times when I doubted my own success. It was through her love and encouragement, and our many late-night mastermind sessions that this book concept was born. She deserves credit for formulating the outline and for helping me capture these strategies and put them into a readable format. She is a successful entrepreneur in her own right (Centerworks.com), and I couldn't ask for a better friend, soul mate, sounding board, and life partner.

I want to thank the great people at John Wiley & Sons, especially Matt Holt, Shannon Vargo, Elana Schulman, and the rest of the team who helped make this book a reality.

Next, I need to thank one of my prosperity thought leaders and close friends, Randy Gage (RandyGage.com). Randy's unabashed prosperity mind-set, combined with his zest for life, is a unique combination. He has created many millionaires through his desire to transform the world by helping people realize their true potential. Over the years, Randy and I have had many heart-to-heart conversations about business, critical thinking, wealth, success, and prosperity.

And my close circle of friends—Steve and Debbie Sims, Will and Phobe Ezell, Robert Smith, Victoria LaBalme, Shep and Cindy Hyken, Michael and Diane Krisa, Mike Foster—all helped along the way, as did my cycling, speed skating, hockey, and poker buddies. All of these people made important contributions. For the past 18 years, I've been a member of the National Speakers Association (NSA) (NSAspeaker.org), an organization filled with experts, thought leaders, professional speakers, authors, and consultants. I'm honored to have served at a national level as a director. I have to acknowledge here that the relationships that resulted from my participation in this association have changed my life for the better on many levels. I've had the opportunity to work with, mentor, and be mentored by a rich talent pool of individuals. Many of them I had known of for years prior to joining NSA.

Imagine my excitement when I was able to hang out with the very same people that I had been listening to on audio, reading their books, or watching on video for years. There have been so many transformational experiences, strategic partners, mastermind sessions, joint ventures, and lessons learned. The really crazy part is when many of my business and success mentors have actually become my clients and close friends. The fact that they sought out my expertise helped to clarify the value I offer through my unique talents, skills, and abilities. I truly learned that the more I learn, the less I really know. What I mean by that is, at this stage of my life, I've finally figured out that there's always more to learn and that practice doesn't make perfection, practice makes improvement. The scariest individuals I know think they know everything but haven't yet figured out what they don't know. I know that may sound confusing, but those people who think they know everything are closed off from new ideas and new opportunities. I know that's not you, or you wouldn't have picked up this book.

I also have to thank my friends and colleagues in the Speakers Roundtable (SpeakersRoundtable.com). This is a who's who of experts, business owners, professional speakers, authors, trainers, and consultants. Collectively, they have published more than

100 books, produced hundreds of audio and video programs, written more than 2,000 published articles, own and run several high-tech and low-tech businesses, and serve as consultants and board members of many well-known corporations. I'm honored to be considered one of their 20 elite members. We are quite an eclectic group. Speakers Roundtable members include Bill Bachrach, Ty Boyd, Jim Cathcart, Danny Cox, Roger Crawford, Bert Decker, Patricia Fripp, Art Holst, Don Hutson, Shep Hyken, Peter Legge, Giovanni Livera, Scott Mckain, Terry Paulson, Charlie Plum, Nido Qubein, Mike Rayburn, Naomi Rhode, Mark Sanborn, Dan Thurman, Jim Tunney, and their spouses.

Acknowledgments also go out to the Entrepreneurs' Organization (EO) (EOnetwork.org), both the Kansas City chapter members and the national EO association. I've presented at many of their local chapters and at a few EO national conferences. It was after presenting a keynote session at their Global Leadership Conference in 2009 that I decided to also become an EO member and join their global network of more than 8,000 business owners and entrepreneurs in over 38 countries. The EO is the catalyst that enables entrepreneurs to learn and grow from each other, leading to greater business success and enriched personal lives. Membership in one of EO's 120 chapters is by invitation only; the average member is 41 years old with annual revenues of $17.3 million.

Special thanks have to go out to my team at Prime Concepts Group, Inc. (PrimeConcepts.com), who've sat through many meetings where I drew my countless mind maps, illustrations, and training concepts: Kasondra Foster, Heather Torres, Leah Osoba, Laura Stow, Paul Badke, Katie Martinez, Ken Gromala, Krista Flying-Out, Tabatha Rourke, Mike Gamache, and Brian Castleberry. As the CEO and leader of such a creative and innovative team, I want to thank you for all of your talents and abilities. You've helped me refine these concepts and practice them in our personal and professional lives. It's in this living laboratory where many of these concepts were refined. Your diverse nature, unique personality styles, generational differences, and educational experience have given the unique insights for delivering the concepts in this book.

My gratitude also goes out to all my clients, audience members, blog readers, and social media tribe members. My clients include small businesses, entrepreneurs, franchisors, major corporations, global entities, and nonprofit organizations. My audience members include top executives, their executive leadership teams, and staff members throughout their organizations. My digital footprint on the Internet includes readership from hundreds of websites. Social media by nature include organic two-way conversations allowing immediate feedback and opinion. As we know, some of the feedback may not be solicited or even wanted, but that doesn't stop people from sharing their thoughts and ideas. With the explosion and expansion of social media sites like Facebook, Twitter, LinkedIn, YouTube, and millions of blogs, it's now easier than ever before to vet new ideas and keep your finger on the pulse of the marketplace. I've included social media in the acknowledgments because the very nature of social networking websites has transformed the way I think, act, and make decisions.

> And when you think about it, isn't that what superpower is really all about? About how we can do more with less, how we can make decisions faster and better, and how we can navigate the new technological landscape of the modern world to produce the results we want in our personal and professional lives?

PART 1

Where Are You Now?

CHAPTER 1

Unlocking Your Superpowers

So you've picked up this book because something about it grabbed you. Was it the catchy title? The promise of getting more out of life with less effort? A desire to take your business into the stratosphere of success? The possibility of overcoming challenges in your personal life that seem to be affecting everything you do?

Are you uncertain about whether your actions are congruent with the results you are getting in life? Do you have goals, know what you want, and have a plan to get there...or have you been struggling with how to make it all happen, better, faster, and with more success?

My goal here is to help get you on track and in tune with your own set of SUPERPOWERS. So everything you want out of life will come true for you...and so you can achieve success in what you want to achieve in every avenue of your life.

THE BIG QUESTION: HOW DO YOU UNLOCK YOUR SUPERPOWERS?

Do you remember asking yourself that question when you were a kid? Did you have a cape and a costume? Did you play the part of Superman, Wonder Woman, Batman, Spiderman, or one of the other heroes who swooped in, thwarted the bad guys, and solved all the world's problems? As kids, we believe in magic, and we have faith that these special skills are real and not just for fairy tales. We believe that we really do have superpowers and, in our childlike minds, have confidence that we can conquer the world.

What happened along the way? Who squashed our beliefs in our own superpowers? Whoever it was (and watch out, it just might have been someone who shows up in the mirror every morning), they forgot how important hero narratives are to human success and achievement. We need to be able to reinvent ourselves as superheroes. It's part of how we're wired as human beings, and we've been doing it for thousands of years. I don't care if your role model was Batman, the Black Panther, or Beowulf. I'm here to tell you that you were on the right track . . . and you need to get back on that track. Regardless of how old you are, where you are in your career, how long you've been in business, or anything else, it's not too late for you to join the ranks of the superhero you loved most, take your power back, and truly conquer your world.

Are you ready to take the first step?

GET STARTED

Take a moment. Find a quiet place. Then close your eyes and see yourself as a superhero. What is your name? What are you wearing? What color is your cape? Do you have a mask? Is there an emblem on your chest? Do you have a magic weapon of some kind, like a sword that starts glowing when the bad guys are approaching from far off? What type of superpowers do you possess? Can you anticipate things before they happen? Have you got X-ray vision? Can you read people's minds? Can you scale tall buildings? Do you have enough strength in one hand to crush a ravenous monster? Can you soar through the air to get a bird's-eye view of your own world?

Whatever these amazing superpowers are that you possess in your mind, we're going to take a look at how you can begin to expand, unlock, develop, and use them in your daily life to get the results you want in your personal life and your business . . . with less effort and a better quality of result in everything you do.

It may sound silly at first to think of yourself as a superhero, but it is the first and most important step in unlocking your power. You must start to see, think, and act differently than you have in the past. The only thing that is constant in life is change. And change is a choice. Choose to get happy about change. If you're not changing, adapting, and growing, it will be a challenge to do new things in different ways to get better results.

Let your superhero self out to play . . . as you begin your journey to greater success!

TAKE A SNAPSHOT OF YOURSELF

Where are you in your life right now? How would you rate yourself on your personal and professional success right now?

Over the years, I've had the privilege of working with many millionaires and even a few billionaires. You would think that people who earn a lot of money would feel successful. I'm sure that many do, but I'm amazed at how many people who fall into that category are still not happy and feel unsuccessful. They are driven to achieve more, to acquire more, to have more, and to do more. They have not yet harnessed their own superpowers.

This morning I got up and started reading a book written by one of my clients, Jean Palmer Heck. The book is *Tough Talks for Tough Times,* a must-read for anybody in management or leadership. There was an illustration and concept she shared about a campaign that Toyota implemented a few years back called "GAME ON." It stands for Gain Advantage, Monetize Everything, Overlook Nothing. That's one of my favorite acronyms, because it showed an entire organization how to harness its untapped superpowers.

In her book, Jean told how Toyota Motor Company launched that initiative throughout the company with the twin goals of reducing fixed costs and increasing top-line revenues. It was a great strategy that saved Toyota more than $235 million! I'm referencing it because it's a great strategy that can be applied to our own lives. I have a few adaptations on the GAME ON concept; here they are.

Gain Advantage

What are you doing to leverage your talents and expertise? Reading this book and applying the concepts is a great step toward taking advantage in your life.

Monetize Everything

How are you managing your money, creating wealth, and using your time?

Overlook Nothing

Are you willing to dig deep and take a good look at *all* of the areas your life? Think about your health and fitness, security and wealth, prosperity consciousness, spirituality, family, social life and relationships, mental development, daily habits and routines, life purpose, and contribution as they relate to your personal and professional life. Just like any trip or journey that you're going to take, you need to know first where you are now, next know where you want to go, and then figure out how you're going to get there. This may sound simple, but that doesn't mean that it's easy.

GAME ON!

It's time to get your GAME ON. It's time to look more closely at what has led you to this moment.

Life has a way of giving us challenges and unforeseen obstacles that create roadblocks on our path to fulfillment and success. How you deal with those obstacles and challenges creates learning experiences that develop your character and personality. Every obstacle you have ever faced, and every response you ever made to those obstacles, directed your path and shaped the superhero you are about to become.

To make that journey, though, you need to know your own starting point. That means taking an assessment of where you are now. We will start this process with you performing a personal assessment and capturing your thoughts and ideas.

As an action step, I'd like you to open up a word-processing document or get a spiral notebook to serve as your personal "Superpower Guidebook." Sure, you could call it a journal or life plan, but I think *Superpower Guidebook* just has a better ring to it. The first step in the superpower process is to get a benchmark of where you are in many areas of your life.

Set aside time on your schedule to write down your perception of where you are in your life right now. This can be an amazing experience if you're honest with yourself and fully immerse yourself into the process. Yes, of course, there's our perspective of ourselves, and there are other people's perspectives of us. For now, I just want you to get your own perspective down on paper or on your word-processing document. I find that when I do this, I go through myriad feelings and states of mind. I feel the entire gamut of emotions, and it's an exhilarating experience.

This Superhero Guidebook is not meant to be part of a scientific process, nor is it a replacement for proper professional help if that is what you need. It is simply a way for you to capture your beliefs as a benchmark in your personal growth process.

Using your Superpower Guidebook or Word document, write answers to the following questions:

Health and Fitness

1. How much do you weigh?
2. How much do you think you should weigh?
3. During a typical week, how many days do you engage in vigorous physical activity for at least 20 minutes?
4. During a typical week, how many days do you engage in mild physical activity for at least 30 minutes at a time?
5. What is your favorite cardio activity?
6. What is your favorite strength-training activity?
7. Do you know your resting heart rate? If so, what is it?

8. On a typical day, how many hours do you watch television, play video games, or use a computer?

9. On a typical day, how many alcoholic drinks, including beer and wine, do you drink?

10. On a typical day, how many soft drinks do you consume?

11. On a scale of 1 to 10, how often do you feel stressed, with 1 being not very much and 10 being daily?

12. Are you taking any medications?

13. Do you take vitamins?

14. On a typical night, how many hours do you sleep?

15. On a scale of 1 to 10, how would you rate your health and fitness, with 1 being poor and 10 being excellent?

Mental Health

1. Do you take the time to meditate, pray, or simply reflect during private time?

2. What are your favorite genres of music?

3. How would you rate your self-talk, that little voice in your head? Is it mostly positive or negative patterns?

4. How much time, if any, during the past month did you feel depressed?

5. During a typical week, do you take time to de-stress?

6. What is your favorite way to relax and de-stress?

7. How much time during the past four weeks have you felt calm and peaceful?

8. On a scale of 1 to 10, how would you rate your energy level, with 1 being low and 10 being lots of energy?

9. Do you consider yourself a good listener?

10. Would others rate you as a good listener?

Career

1. Do you work for someone else, or are you self-employed?
2. What is your position title?
3. How do you describe what you do to your friends and family?
4. Do you manage other people?
5. Are you an executive, manager, or staff person?
6. How many different companies have you worked for?
7. Is your career mentally stimulating or boring?
8. Do you like what you do?
9. What are the top three skill sets required for success in your position?
10. How would you rate yourself on the performance of those skill sets (1 to 10, with 1 being poor and 10 being excellent)?
11. Are you getting paid what you're worth?
12. What are you doing to keep your skill sets current each year?

Wealth and Financial Security

1. Do you use a program like Quicken® to track and manage your finances?
2. How much money do you earn each year?
3. How much money do you save each year?
4. How much money do you invest each year?
5. How much debt do you have?
6. Amount of short-term debt (credit cards, loans, etc.)?
7. Amount of long-term debt (mortgage, business loans, etc.)?
8. Your total assets?
9. Your total liabilities?
10. Do you have a retirement plan, a 401(k) or IRA?

11. Do you have health and life insurance?

12. Do you live on a budget, or do you make your financial decisions without any budget?

Relationships

1. Who are your top five friends? Why?

2. Who is your best friend? Why?

3. Are you in an intimate relationship?

4. Rate those relationships on scale of 1 to 10, with 1 being poor and 10 being outstanding.

5. Are you single, married, or divorced? (circle one)

6. Are you a parent?

7. How social do you consider yourself to be (on a scale of 1 to 10)?

Spirituality

1. Do you consider yourself spiritual or religious?

2. Do you believe in a higher power?

3. Do you follow any spiritual path or practice (e.g., meditation, yoga, chanting)?

4. What have been your most important experiences, if any, concerning your relationship with God or your higher power?

5. What things do you believe in that give meaning to your life?

6. What would you say is your purpose in life?

For additional insights into your personality and way of thinking, you may want to explore the professional assessments from DISC®, McQuaig Surveys®, Emotional Intelligence™ (EI), or the whole-brain model from Herrmann International. These tools can help you identify your strengths and weaknesses while outlining a road map for improvement.

Knowing others is intelligence; knowing yourself is true wisdom.
Mastering others is strength; mastering yourself is true power.

—Anonymous

Confront the dark parts of yourself, and work to banish them with illumination and forgiveness. Your willingness to wrestle with your demons will cause your angels to sing. Use the pain as fuel, as a reminder of your strength.

— August Wilson

The final mystery is oneself.

—Oscar Wilde

Trust yourself. You know more than you think you do.

—Benjamin Spock

A man should first direct himself in the way he should go. Only then should he instruct others.

—Buddha

One must know oneself. If this does not serve to discover truth, it at least serves as a rule of life, and there is nothing better.

—Blaise Pascal

Self-reverence, self-knowledge, self-control—these three alone lead to power.

—Alfred, Lord Tennyson

We know what we are, but know not what we may be.

— William Shakespeare

Ninety percent of the world's woe comes from people not knowing themselves, their abilities, their frailties, and even their real virtues. Most of us go almost all the way through life as complete strangers to ourselves.

— Sydney J. Harris

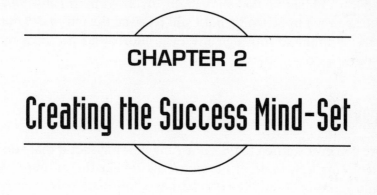

CHAPTER 2

Creating the Success Mind-Set

Okay, let's get down to business and talk about your BS. Relax . . . I'm talking about your BELIEF SYSTEM.

What you believe about yourself and your world and how you think have a powerful effect on what you are able to achieve and accomplish. Do you see yourself as a creative and innovative thinker? Do you like yourself? Are you proud of the things you've accomplished in life so far? Do you have a can-do attitude? Or do your belief systems create roadblocks and limitations that prevent you from accessing your superpowers?

I was at a business growth meeting a while ago, and one of the presenters was Bonnie McElveen-Hunter. She's ambassador for the United States to Finland; she's also president and CEO of Pace Communications and chairman of the American Red Cross. Talk about a superhero! This amazing woman continues to use her superpowers both for business success and to make a positive impact on the planet. When asked what has helped her become the superwoman she is today, she said, "When I was a child, my mother made me write the words 'I can't' on a piece of paper, put it in a shoebox, and bury it in the backyard. The words 'I can't' have never been a part of my vocabulary. My only option is 'I can' . . . then I just have to figure out a way to make it happen."

Wow! How fabulous to have a parent insightful enough to help a child learn to believe that she can do anything! Personally, I wasn't so lucky in my upbringing, but I still received the gift of developing a success mind-set through my own efforts and the help of my mentors.

"I CAN"

Have you ever wanted to do something new but found that you just weren't sure how to do it? I think we all feel like this at times. What would you suppose holds us back from taking action? Is it our belief system, our programming, or our conditioning? Is it a combination of all three?

We're talking about the transition from "I can't" to "I can." For a superhero (and for a successful entrepreneur), that's just common sense. My working title for this book was *Common Sense Is a Superpower*. Common sense seems to have been the foundation for everything I've done and achieved in my life. When I talk to other people about common sense, however, they tell me that my common sense isn't all that common.

I've been an entrepreneur since I was 12 years old, when I started my car-washing business. All I needed was the hose, a bucket, some dish soap, and some dirty cars. The summers were hot, and the winters were freezing in Minneapolis, Minnesota, so this was definitely a seasonal business. I was in sixth grade, and I washed cars after school. I was fascinated about how easy it was to make money. Of course, for a 12-year-old, even $20 seems like a lot of money, or at least it did back in the 1970s. I was adopted into a single-parent home, lived in foster homes and detention centers, and spent much of my time on my own running around the streets.

At 15 years old, I found myself living in the government housing projects in North Minneapolis, paying $17 a month for rent. Don't get me wrong. I didn't miss any meals, and many people had it much worse than I did. I was also on the work program throughout high school. This means I had to go to school for only one hour a day to check in in the morning and then go to work. My employer then filled out my report card, and it counted as credit for my grade. Here's where it gets really cool. I decided that if I was my own boss, I could fill out my own report card and have control over my life. (I'm sharing this background information with you as a foundation so you can get a sense of my "I can" thought processes back then — and today, too.)

At 15 years old, I was trying to figure out how to make money in different ways than everybody else in my neighborhood. I remember sitting down with the Yellow Pages phone book, looking at all the businesses, and trying to decide which type of business I could run. I knew it had to be something fairly easy that didn't take a lot of money to get started. As I came across the *P*, I landed on "painting."

That was it. I would start a painting company. Why? Because I had spent a fair amount of time in detention centers, and as punishment for swearing, they made us paint the walls. Surprise, surprise: I became a decent painter . . . or at least I thought I was.

I went to my friends at school who were in shop class and asked them to make me up some flyers that said "Saeks Painting and Light Construction." I added "light construction" as a way to make it easier to get jobs. It was light construction because I didn't have any construction experience. My buddy Steve Sims created the logo, and I printed up business cards.

So there I was. I thought I was in business because I had flyers and business cards. Forget the fact that I didn't have any customers, any equipment, or any real business experience. I handed out those flyers and business cards everywhere I could think of. I put them on car windshields in parking lots and on grocery store bulletin boards, and I handed them out on street corners.

During this same period, I was working as a cashier in the Army Surplus Store on Fourth Street and Hennepin Avenue in downtown Minneapolis. Each night after work, I checked my answering machine to see if it had any lead calls from my flyers. Finally, I saw the light on the answering machine blinking! I was so excited. Just what I wanted: a real, live lead! My excitement soon turned to fear and anxiety, as I realized that I didn't have even a clue on how to write a proposal for a painting job.

My self-talk kicked in. "You can't do that, you're not smart enough, you're not old enough, you don't have enough experience, you don't have any money, what are you thinking?" Now at the time, I didn't know what self-talk was. I heard just that little voice in my head trying to hold me back.

Sound familiar? How many times in your life have you been faced with an opportunity, only to let the little voice in your head hold you back or talk you out of it?

I knew I needed help, so I went down to the local paint store on 29th and Bryant Avenue. I walked in and saw that the store was very busy, so I went right up to the desk and asked for the manager. The man behind the counter said he was the manager, and I jumped in by telling him that I just started a new painting services business and that I needed his help with a new proposal. He took one look at me and said, "Kid, get the hell out my store."

I didn't realize how foolish I must've looked with my long hair and my army jacket; I also had a 9mm handgun in my back pocket. But I was persistent; I didn't have anything to lose because I was working for $1.10 an hour at the surplus store. I didn't leave. I kept asking him for his help.

Eventually, he said, "Okay, kid, I'll help you."

He went over to the shelf and grabbed a quart of paint and a paintbrush. He opened up that paint can and got that brush out and started splashing paint all over my clothes and shoes. I said, "What the hell are you doing?" He said, "Well, you didn't look like a painter, but now you do." He then gave me a painter's cap, a calculator, and some instructions. Then, God bless him, he sent me on my way to the prospect's house.

It was an older two-story home, with a nice groomed lawn in the south part of Minneapolis. Now I had two little voices with sound tracks playing in my head: one voice telling me to go for it and one trying to convince me that I was crazy. Thank God, I listened to the right voice and knocked on the door.

16

A nice man in his 50s opened the door, and he smiled at me. I shook his hand and explained that I was there to gather the information to prepare the proposal. He walked me from room to room, explaining what he wanted to have painted. In the kitchen, he wanted the walls KILZed and the windows glazed. In the hallways, he wanted to have semigloss paint; in the bedrooms, he wanted flat paint; in the bathroom, he wanted gloss paint. Then he pointed at the ceilings where they were cracked around the ceiling fans and said he wanted me to fix the ceilings and paint them. Now I was way over my head.

I didn't know what KILZ meant or what glazing windows meant. I thought paint is paint. I didn't know flat from semigloss or oil-based from water-based paint. I measured the size of each room and wrote everything down. I explained to the man that I had to go back to my office to prepare the proposal and that I would be back in about an hour. Right, my office. I didn't even own a paintbrush yet. Back at the paint store, the manager helped me calculate all of the supplies and equipment that I would need for the job. He gave me suggestions on how much to charge and how to prepare the proposal.

I jumped back in my car and headed back to the prospect's house. This time when I knocked on the door and the door opened, the man's wife was with him. She took one look at me and stepped right behind her husband. I remember thinking, "This isn't going to go well."

With my heart pounding, I handed them the proposal and said, "The price for this job is $1,025, and I need 50 percent up front as a deposit, with 50 percent due on completion." The man looked at me, then at the quote, and then back at me and said, "Do you have any experience?"

This was a critical point in my new line of work and in my career. Do I explain to this nice couple that my only experience was repainting the entire north wing of the Hennepin County Detention Center? No, being quick on my feet, I explained that if they weren't 100 percent satisfied with the finished job, they would receive a full refund, with no questions asked. The woman turned to her husband and said, "Honey, write him a check."

He did.

I sat in my car—which, by the way, had no insurance, tags, or title—looking at that check for $525 for a very long time. That was more money than I would earn working at the Army surplus store for over a month. The deposit money was enough for me to buy initial supplies and start-up equipment, but I needed help to complete this job.

It was the end of October, and the weather was already starting to turn cold. I stood outside the paint store in sleeting rain asking each person entering the store if they were looking for paint work. Finally, after three hours, a small crew of painters said yes, they would help me out. I gave them 60 percent and I kept 40 percent. We kept the customer satisfied. And I got to keep the money I made.

By the end of my first year in my business, I had three painting crews working for me, and their average age was 40. I earned more than $35,000 that first year. Not bad for a juvenile in the late 1970s. In today's economy, that amount would equate to over $150,000.

A side note: Do you want to guess what happens when a kid from the projects gets $35,000? Right. He spends $36,000. It took a few years for me to understand business operations, finance and accounting, inventory control, and direct-response marketing and to refine my sales skills.

All this was a long time ago. For many years, I had a chip on my shoulder for growing up without any parental guidance or true formal education. That chip splintered away over time, though, as I read new books, listened to new audio programs, attended seminars, and made some better distinctions in my life. My point is that you can do the same. And you can turn off the "I can't" voice and listen to the "I can" voice any time you choose.

That is the foundational element of this book. The difference between your superhero and where you are right now can be measured by the choices you make, right now, about what you believe you can and can't do. I'm sharing my experiences and insights here not to convince you about how wonderful I am—believe me, lots of people have better stories than I do—but to help you get some traction when it comes to thinking, acting, and performing in accordance with your best and highest self. That's the first step to getting more done with less effort and producing better results.

The great successful men of the world have used their imagination; they think ahead and create their mental picture in all its details, filling in here, adding a little there, altering this a bit and that a bit, but steadily building—steadily building.

—Robert Collier

Success doesn't come to you. You go to it.

—Marva Collins

The difference between a successful person and others is not a lack of strength, not a lack of knowledge, but rather in a lack of will.

—Vincent T. Lombardi

The best way to predict your future is to create it.

—Stephen Covey

What lies behind us, and what lies before us are tiny matters, compared to what lies within us.

—Ralph Waldo Emerson

If you are distressed by anything external, the pain is not due to the thing itself but to your own estimate of it; and this you have the power to revoke at any moment.

—Marcus Aurelius

If you can dream it, you can do it.

—Walt Disney

You miss 100% of the shots you don't take.

—Wayne Gretzky

Whatever the mind can conceive and believe, the mind can achieve.

—Napoleon Hill

Here are three things you can do right now to start shifting your mind-set for superpower success.

1. Put yourself first on the list of things to do. If you don't take care of yourself, you won't have the energy to take care of anyone or anything else.

2. Recognize that your thoughts determine your beliefs, beliefs determine your behaviors, your behaviors determine your habits and actions, and your habits and actions lead to your results. If you want better results, then you need to make sure that your beliefs, behaviors, habits, and actions are in alignment with your goals.

3. Write in your Superpower Guidebook at least a few times each week, if not daily, to record your feelings and progress.

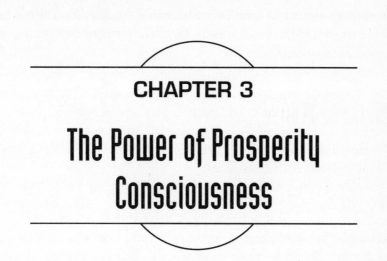

CHAPTER 3

The Power of Prosperity Consciousness

Are you living in lack or abundance? Are you part of the scarcity herd, or are you in that tiny 2 percent or so of the population that knows how important prosperity consciousness is for success?

Being prosperity-minded is definitely a superpower. I first heard the term *prosperity consciousness* from my friend and business partner, Randy Gage. I credit Randy with introducing me to the tools, teachings, and tactics to replace *lack consciousness* with the power of *prosperity consciousness*.

You may have heard the saying "What you focus on you attract." A few years ago, there was a popular book and DVD movie titled *The Secret*. It was an inspirational teaching to the general public introducing time-tested strategies for success and repackaging them to be more current. The basic concept with the book centered around the concept of the law of attraction. It received millions in publicity and sold in many languages around the world. So I'm not so sure it really was a secret . . . but it certainly was to the masses. It's very similar to the quote by Henry Ford, "If you think you can . . . you can. And if you think you can't . . . you can't." But the concept of just thinking and focusing on what you want to attract alone is not enough to create true prosperity in your life. You must take conscious action in your mind, self-talk, positive behaviors, and massive action steps.

WHAT IS PROSPERITY?

This is a tricky question. Prosperity is much more than creating monetary wealth. Prosperity can manifest itself in many different ways. For some people, it's creating wealth and measuring that prosperity by collecting material things; for others, it's peace of mind, happiness, and spirituality. I believe that prosperity is how you look at the world and everything around you. It manifests itself in your mind and in your thoughts. It's not something external, and you can experience prosperity at any level of income, at any time of day or night, specifically including now. I certainly don't consider myself a prosperity guru. I'm just a person wanting to improve my life and create wealth and abundance for myself and for as many people and organizations as I can help. I help people through my books, blogs, keynote presentations, and consultations. You help people however you choose to help them. Most people think life forces them to make choices. I have a different view: I think your choices make your life. Or more specifically, you make the choices—and then your choices make you. Your wealth, health, and outlook—all the different forms of prosperity you are living or not living today—are the result of the choices you've made up to this point. Every day is a new day, and even every minute is a new minute. You can make a choice to change at any time. Choose prosperity. You're worth it.

WHAT IS YOUR RELATIONSHIP WITH MONEY?

Do you think earning money is evil or bad? Do you believe that wealthy people did something devious to create it? If you listen to the mainstream media, that's what you will hear pretty regularly.

Many TV shows portray the wealthy person as the villain or the oddball. Don't take my word for it; just watch your TV shows, and you'll see how most wealthy people are usually set up as the bad guys. Now, if you consider that most people may watch TV from four to six hours each day, imagine the negative programming that you are bombarded with after a week, a month, 10 years, or throughout your life history. Imagine the impact it would have on your own attitudes about money. Imagine how it would affect your ability to create wealth, prosperity, and abundance in your own life.

You are meant to be healthy, happy, and prosperous. Once you recognize and accept this, it is simply a case of learning the principles that abundance is based on. To help you offset past negative programming or your lack consciousness and supercharge your path to prosperity, I'm going to practice the circulation law of prosperity and give you a free immediate download of Randy Gage's popular Prosperity Series. These are short, easy-to-read books—enjoy them.

In this insightful series, you will move from lack consciousness to living in the light of true abundance. Randy Gage reveals:

- What creates prosperity consciousness
- The universal laws that govern prosperity
- Why you should embrace critical thinking
- The secret to creating a vacuum for good
- What it takes to manifest prosperity on the physical plane
- Why you are supposed to be wealthy

The five-book series includes:

101 Keys to Your Prosperity
Accept Your Abundance! Why You are Supposed to Be Wealthy
37 Secrets About Prosperity
Prosperity Mind! How to Harness the Power of Thought
The 7 Spiritual Laws of Prosperity

You can claim your Prosperity Series books at www.prime concepts.com/superpower/prosperity.

I've been an entrepreneur as far back as I can remember. I've been self-employed the majority of my life, but let's explore a story about one of my few corporate career positions. It was January 1984, and I was cold-calling on businesses to sell commercial carpet cleaning services for my company, Saeks Carpet Cleaning Services. After securing a new contract to clean several locations of the Fox Meyer Drug Company with the director of operations, he asked me if I knew anything about computers. Back then, computers filled entire floors of office buildings. There were a few personal computers, but mostly, when you said, "computer," you were talking about very large pieces of equipment. I was always fascinated by technology and had played around with a VIC-20 and a Commodore Amiga computer. Looking back, I realize these were hardly sophisticated computers: no hard drives, no fancy graphics, just the keyboard that connected to your TV set. I asked him what he was looking for, and he said, "We're looking for smart, talented people that can help us train pharmacists how to use our new software, and I think you can help."

Over the next hour and a half, he outlined the new position to me and offered me a job. I was already self-employed, but I thought this would be fun and I'd learn a lot. I had carpet cleaning crews in place in my company, so I took the position.

Over the next three years, I traveled across the country helping hundreds of pharmacists from Kmart stores learn how to use computers to manage patient records, manage drug inventory, and print reports. I became a train-the-trainer for hiring and teaching new installers and trainers, and I became popular for taking complicated subjects and making them easier to understand. My salary and benefits kept increasing, and I advanced through the ranks to the senior buyer of data processing for more than 65 divisions, managing a multimillion-dollar budget. I was on the fast track to a long-term career, or at least I thought I was.

You see, there was a gentleman who was the current director of purchasing (I'll call him Bill) who had held that position for over

30 years, and now I was offered his job. He was 65 years old, and the company policy was mandatory retirement. I was supposed to train with him for 90 days prior to his retirement, but when I came to him on day one of the training, he said, "Kid, I've worked here half of my life, and I'll be damned if I'm going to train you to take over my position. Go find something to do, and you can take over the position on my last day."

The 90 days went fast. On his last day, I went into his office, and I watched him put down his pencil on his notepad, picked up his overcoat, and put on his hat and walked out of the office. No going-away party, no special celebration—he just gathered his few belongings and walked out of the office.

At first, I was excited by the new position and sat down in the chair at his desk in elation. Then it hit me: Was that what I was in store for? Dedicating 30 years or more of my life to a company, only to leave one day in quiet desperation, didn't seem that exciting. There I was in the cold office trying to picture the future, and all I could think about was the look on Bill's face as he left his office for the last time. He looked sad and depleted.

I didn't sleep much that night. The next day I went to the executive director's office and resigned. He tried to convince me to stay and said that I would never find a better job, especially since I didn't have a college degree. He went on a guilt trip about how I had been given advances faster than other people who had been at the company longer than I had. He said I should appreciate all he had done for me. What he didn't understand is that I have a belief that "somebody else's opinion is not my reality. I was appreciative, but I had also given a lot of value to the company, and I had nothing to be ashamed of for this decision. He tried to convince me to stay, but my mind was set on leaving. On the drive home from the office, I did have second thoughts, but then I saw Bill's face in my mind, and I knew I had made the right decision.

Now what? I still had a fair income from my carpet-cleaning business but couldn't see myself cleaning carpets the rest of my life either. I was sitting in my two-bedroom apartment looking at my expensive Italian racing bicycles leaning up against the wall. I thought, "I need to clean up my life, and I am going to start with this apartment."

Where was I to put those racing bicycles? I could have put them out on the balcony, but beside the fact that they could easily be stolen, these were works of art. My next choice was to drill holes in the ceiling and install metal hooks to hang the bikes, but then I would lose my damage deposit. That wasn't an option, so what was I going to do with those bikes? I knew I wasn't the only person storing bikes in limited space. All of the other bicycle racers I knew had at least two or three bicycles, not to mention kids in college dorms, everyone living in apartments, and then the overseas market opportunities. I realized I had identified not a problem, but an opportunity. It's interesting how, when you start to focus on a problem, your mind can work to help you resolve the situation. I'm not talking about focusing on negativity; I'm referring to focusing on a challenge and asking yourself questions that help your mind come up with solutions. There I was, semi-unemployed, and looking toward the future of possibilities.

There were two little voices in my head, one saying, "Congratulations on having the courage to leap and grow your wings on the way down," and the other voice in my head saying, "You idiot, why did you just leave a job with a great salary and benefits?" I bet you can relate to the situation. I know there've been times in your life when you had to make a tough decision and your self-talk talked you either into it or out of it. In my heart of hearts, I knew I'd made the right decision. I just didn't know exactly what I was going to do next—at least not until I started thinking about those bikes.

I grabbed a notepad and started sketching out devices that could store my bicycles. The criteria were that it needed to protect the bikes and also protect the interior of my apartment. After a couple of hours of drawing on paper, I had a rough sketch of a floor-to-ceiling bicycle rack that would use tension to secure it into place. The next day I took the drawing to a woodcraft shop and asked them to build me a prototype. They said it would cost $65. I was very excited. A week later they called, and I picked up the prototype. It was a solid oak bicycle storage rack with interlocking pieces that enabled it to adjust to different ceiling heights with furniture levelers at the bottom to manually adjust the tension. I installed it as soon as I got home, and it worked perfectly. I thought about the millions of bicycle owners and that if I could reach a percentage of them and get them to purchase this product, I could earn millions.

My dream of starting another business was born. Having been an avid reader of motivational quote books for inspiration and insights, several of the popular quotes were going through my head:

- If you think you can . . . you can. If you think you can't . . . you can't. (Henry Ford)
- Luck is where preparation meets opportunity. (Earl Nightingale)
- Try not to become a man of success but a man of value. (Albert Einstein)
- Every artist was first an amateur. (Ralph Waldo Emerson)
- Far better is it to dare mighty things, to win glorious triumphs, even though checkered by failure . . . than to rank with those poor spirits who neither enjoy nor suffer much, because they live in a gray twilight that knows not victory nor defeat. (Theodore Roosevelt)
- Go out and buy yourself a 5-cent pencil and a 10-cent notebook and begin to write down some million-dollar ideas for yourself. (Bob Grinde)

Back to the notepad I went, capturing all of my ideas and evaluating the new business opportunity. How would I manufacture them, where would I get the investment capital, how could I market and sell them, and how much money could I make? This was in 1984, and using the Internet was not an option. I went to a few business consulting firms for advice and insights, and all of them said that I had a short-term business life. Why, might you ask? They said that the product selling for $189 would be too expensive and that the competition was a 99-cent hook. They said I would saturate the market within three years and then be out of business.

(Flash forward insight: I've been a business grow strategist now for over 20 years, and having helped thousands of entrepreneurs, organizations, and businesses grow over the past 20 years, I'm always conscious of how those other business consultants were so adamant about their opinions but couldn't have been more wrong. So as much as I am myself very opinionated with my insights and expertise, I'm conscious of the fact that in business, you have to take calculated risks, along with testing, research, market feedback, and being open to new ideas. Now we return to the bicycle storage rack business story.)

I hired an intellectual property and patent attorney to file U.S. patents on my invention. There went another $15,000 of my savings. Patents are a funny thing, as I learned later that they really may not protect much at all, just give you the right to protect and uphold your patent in a court of law. However, they were a big asset years later, when I sold the company. By the way, this is not an attempt at giving you legal advice. I'm only sharing my perspective, having spent many thousands of dollars on attorneys' fees, patents, copyrights, and trademarks.

My first adventure in selling my product was to promote it directly to other bicycle racers and recreational cyclists at the larger bicycle events. I traveled across the country, setting up a mobile display out of my bronze 1980 Chevy van on a street corner and handing out flyers at the event starting and finish lines. In the first 90 days, I sold only about 20 units, and the conversion ratios sucked. I hardly made enough money to break even on the trips. Next, I cold-called bicycle dealers to try to convince them to carry the product in their stores. Many of them were willing to take the bike racks on consignment . . . but I needed cash flow. It was now almost six months into this new business venture, and I had depleted all of my savings. I knew there just had to be a better way. I knew there were people who would purchase it if I could just get the right combination of marketing message, target market, and marketing method.

I knew I was making it too hard, and then it hit me: I wasn't using my common sense superpower. I wasn't listening enough.

Over the next two weeks, instead of trying to convince bicycle dealers to carry my products, I interviewed them on where they purchased their products, how they made their buying decisions, what trade shows they went to, what magazines they read, and which vendors they purchased from and why. Then I called those vendors and interviewed them to determine their channels of distribution, which trade shows they went to, and how they manufactured, marketed, and sold their products. It was amazing how all of the pieces of how to transform my fledgling small business started to come into absolute focus. This was a great decision and reminded me of another quote, "Good judgment comes from experience. And experience comes from bad judgment" (Mulla Nasrudin). My initial strategy wasn't totally flawed nor an example of bad judgment, but I would have been better served if I had decided to reevaluate the strategy and results sooner.

To make a long story short, the research revealed a bicycle trade show in Long Beach coming up in just three weeks. I had to be there; I knew this would be the ticket to my success. I called the Interbike trade show offices to find out about exhibiting at the convention. The salesperson laughed at me and said I was crazy to think that I could get booth space three weeks before a show that sells out at least a year in advance and has a waiting list. I wasn't going to be denied and knew that there just had to be a way I could exhibit at that show. By now, I had formed a great relationship with the wood manufacturing shop that was producing my wooden storage bike racks. I convinced them to help me make a display that would simulate a floor and ceiling where I could display the bike racks at the show. One way or another, I was going to be exhibiting in Long Beach, California.

I packed up my van with all the supplies, the makeshift trade show booth, and my friend Steve Sims, and we started the drive from Wichita, Kansas, to the West Coast. My plan was to show up and see if there were any exhibitor booth cancellations; if not, then I would attend the show and use it as another opportunity to research the media and the marketplace. It was a long drive, especially with a two-day detour to Las Vegas, but we made it to the convention hotel just in time for the setup days of the trade show.

As it turned out, though, the salesperson had been right: I was crazy to think I could get a booth at what was the largest bicycle-related trade show in the United States at the last moment. My persistence got the best of me, and I wasn't ready to quit, give up, and go home. I knew if I could just get in front of the right people and show them the creative products I had invented, I would have a successful venture. So here's what Steve and I did.

We waited until 2 A.M. on the last setup night and carried all of our supplies and the trade show booth into the lobby area of the hotel, where registration would take place. There, without permission, we set up our 10-by-10 booth outside the main doors of the convention center. This was right across from the double doors entering the main trade show hall, and it was completely against the rules. I figured the worst they could do was kick us out.

The next morning we put on our suits, made our way to the lobby, turned on the lights on the booth, arranged all the flyers on a table, and looked ready for business. As people started to filter in to the registration area, *not one person from the Interbike staff even asked us what we thought we were doing!*

There were so many people at the registration area trying to get their name badges and so many exhibitors trying to get last-minute accessories for their booth that I guess they were too busy to worry about us. This was a three-day show, and we thought certainly we would get kicked out at some point. But we didn't. You want to know something else? We couldn't have asked for a better location, because everybody entering and exiting the trade show floor had to walk directly by our booth. Other exhibitors complimented us on our booth location, and we had tons of foot traffic.

The first two days, we handed out thousands of brochures about our products, and we took wholesale orders for a few hundred bicycle storage units. We were excited, but certainly a couple of hundred bike racks was way under our target, especially with the thousands of dealers at the trade show. Several of the bicycle magazines took pictures and interviewed us for new product reviews, and we received interest from import-export agencies, manufacturer's reps, chain stores, and specialty catalogs.

At the end of the second day, traffic had really slowed down, and we were thinking that if the second day was slow, the third day would be even slower. We would give it until noon to evaluate the traffic, and if it was slow, we would pack up and start the drive home early. On the third day, the morning traffic was slow, and at 11:30 A.M., we started to pack boxes. Just as we started packing, a dealer walked up and handed us an order for 25 bike racks. We stopped packing, took the order, and thanked the man. A minute later, another dealer walked up and handed us his order, and then another and another and another order came rolling in. Steve and I were swamped, taking hundreds of orders from bicycle dealers and chain stores for the next five hours until the end of the show. We ended up with over $100,000 in new orders. (We learned something new about trade shows with this experience: Sometimes people hold off placing their orders until the last day. I'll tell you more about that in a minute.)

Of course, that big influx of orders created a whole host of other issues, for example, production capacity, cash-flow concerns, growing business operations and infrastructure, publicity, marketing, packaging, and distribution, just to name a few—but we were up and running.

Had I left early as planned, I would have missed the number one opportunity to grow and develop my business. That business generated over $40 million in sales before I sold it in 1994. There are several important lessons here, the most important of which, I think, is don't listen to "I can't" self-talk or quit too soon on your dreams.

On a more specific note, here's a breakdown on what happened with the trade show timing. It was a three-day show: Thursday, Friday, and Saturday, all day. On Thursday and Friday (days one and two) of the trade show, the dealers walk around from booth to booth collecting information, researching new products, and connecting with current vendors. On Friday afternoon (day two), the traffic slows down as the dealers go back to their hotels to meet with their staff members, evaluate new products, and write out their purchase orders. On Friday night, they go out and party or spend time with their families, they finalize their orders on Saturday morning, and then they come back to the trade show Saturday afternoon (day three) to place their purchase orders with the vendors of choice. I sure am glad that we didn't leave early!

GETTING BETTER ALL THE TIME

Creating prosperity consciousness is not a one-time activity. It's a lifelong practice. And it's not just about financial wealth.

We are typically surrounded by so much negativity and lack programming and so influenced by our environment, ethnicity, childhood upbringing, families, friends, coworkers, and society that it's not something that gets fixed and then you forget it. It's something that takes work, and regardless of what level of prosperity consciousness you reach, there are always new levels to reach for and achieve.

Formal education will make you a living; self-education will make you a fortune.
— *Jim Rohn*

I am no longer cursed by poverty because I took possession of my own mind, and that mind has yielded me every material thing I want, and much more than I need. But this power of mind is a universal one, available to the humblest person as it is to the greatest.
—*Andrew Carnegie*

What power this is I cannot say. All that I know is that it exists.
—*Alexander Graham Bell*

You create your own universe as you go along.
— *Winston Churchill*

All that we are is the result of what we have thought.
—*Buddha*

Man must cease attributing his problems to his environment, and learn again to exercise his will—his personal responsibility.

—Albert Schweitzer

Take the first step in faith. You don't have to see the whole staircase, just take the first step.

—Martin Luther King Jr.

Action Steps to Develop Your Prosperity Consciousness Superpower

1. Get your free immediate download of Randy Gage's popular Prosperity Series and read them: www.primeconcepts .com/superpower/prosperity.

2. Reduce the number of hours you now spend watching TV by 50 percent or more for at least 30 days . . . and notice how you'll naturally spend your time more productively.

3. Make a list of all the people in your life that you spend time with on a regular basis. These might be family members, coworkers, associates, or friends. Give them a prosperity consciousness rating on a scale of 1 to 10, with 1 being lack consciousness or generally negative and 10 being generally positive and highly supportive of positive activities, thoughts, and behaviors. Make a conscious effort to eliminate spending time with the negative people in your life, and invest your time with people of prosperity consciousness. This exercise can be a real eye-opener.

4. Schedule time each week to read, watch, and/or listen to personal growth and development resources. You'll find that even resources that you may be familiar with from the past have new insights as you grow and develop.

5. Use your Superpower Guidebook to track your thoughts, feelings, actions, and results. Look for patterns of positivity and cynicism; identify your most common attitudes and outlooks. Take control of them.

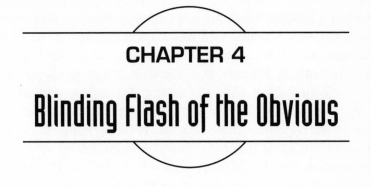

CHAPTER 4

Blinding Flash of the Obvious

As I mentioned earlier, I originally wanted the title of this book to be *Common Sense Is a Superpower!* That's something I say at a lot of my live programs, and it leads me to an important question: How often do you actually listen to your own common sense?

That's the instinctive little voice inside your head that gives you advice, ideas, and inspiration—that is, when you're tuned in to listen to the channel. Dozens of times a day, we have the experience of having a thought or idea that might seem so simple, yet it can transform everything . . . unless we fail to see it , capture it, or follow through on it.

When Columbus sailed to America, they say, the Native Americans didn't notice the ships on the horizon . . . *because they had never seen ships.* Common sense would have challenged one Native American to ask another, "What the heck is that out there?" It's time to develop your skills to the next level to think outside the box or, as a good friend of mine, Nido Qubein, says, "to throw the box outside the window." Learning to trust and use your God-given common sense to think, act, and react *is* a superpower!

HARNESSING THE COMMON SENSE SUPERPOWER: A TRUE STORY

I love being around water for relaxation, recreation, and exercise. In the late 1990s, I owned a 28-foot Bayliner cabin-cruiser boat on El Dorado Lake. The lake was small compared to the large lakes I grew up with in Minnesota. I loved to spend weekends at the lake—cruising, fishing, and just relaxing. At the time, my son Logan was only five years old, and we wanted to keep him safe. So whenever he was on the boat, he was wearing one of those orange horse-collar life jackets. He hated it because it was uncomfortable and hard to swim in. Some people say that a boat is just a hole in the water you throw your money into, but I saw it as an oasis of relaxation and was always looking for new boating accessories.

One weekend, Logan and I attended a large consumer boating show at Century II convention center in Wichita, Kansas. As we walked up and down the aisles, looking at the new gadgets and new boats, something exciting caught my eye. The sign said, "Floating Swimwear: Protect Your Kids in and around Water." I walked right up to the booth, a simple 10-by-10 display, and on the table were colorful Lycra swimsuits with floatation material sewn into them at the back. The patterns were quite colorful and bright, and even Logan was interested. In my mind I was thinking, this is going to be perfect, it replaces the life jacket, and it's something he'll wear that's comfortable and safe.

I told the man behind the table that I wanted to purchase two of them, and his response shocked me a bit. He said, "Don't you want to know how much they cost?" It shocked me because of my entrepreneurial marketing mind-set. I wasn't concerned about how much they cost; I was concerned about keeping Logan safe and enjoying my weekend on the lake. I quickly concluded that the guy working the table didn't really know a lot about marketing or sales.

The suits were $35 each, and I wrote him a check. As I took a few steps away from the table, I stopped, turned, walked back to the table, handed him my business card, and said, "If you'd like to get some help on how to grow your business and expand nationally and internationally, let me know." I was wearing shorts and a T-shirt, not my business suit, but I explained to him that I was the CEO of an integrated marketing company and founder of a sporting goods manufacturing company. He said, "Thanks, but no thanks! If I had a nickel for everybody who offered me help and said that I could make millions with this product I would've retired long ago."

I thought to myself, you can lead a horse to water, but you can't make him drink. I drove back to the lake with Logan to enjoy what was left of the weekend and to try out the new floating swimwear swimsuits for Logan. He loved the swimsuit and said it made him feel like Superman. He could jump in the water, and his head would pop right up. He could swim and play, and he enjoyed wearing it even on the boat or while we were at the marina. Everyone who saw Logan in the suit complimented him on how cool it was and asked where they could get one, too. After answering the question for what seemed like 1,000 times, I had an idea.

We jumped in my truck and drove back to Century II. I went up to the man at the floating swimwear booth and said, "I'd like to buy the entire inventory you have. What kind of deal can you make me?" He said, "I can't sell you my entire inventory because there are two more days left in the boat show." Now I really understood this guy needed help. There I was standing in front of him and offering to buy all of his swimsuits, and what he was thinking about was standing behind an eight-foot table in a 10-by-10 booth eating stale hot dogs while trying to sell suits one at a time . . . instead of selling them all to me in one bulk order.

We finally made a deal that I could purchase all of the suits on hand for $25 each, and I loaded up the truck with several boxes. I drove back to the marina at El Dorado Lake, where I made a deal with the marina manager to give me shelf space and split the profits, allowing me to sell the suits as an impulse purchase item. There were shelves right next to the cash register that held potato chips and candy bars. I moved those items to a different shelf and lined up a few suits across the top shelf, along with a makeshift handmade sign: "Floating Swimwear suits: $50 each while supplies last." It only took two weeks to sell the entire inventory, and that was at a fairly small marina.

All I could think about was how many marinas, boating stores, and pool and spa dealers there were in the United States and the world. I needed more inventory and called the Floating Swimwear owner to get more swimsuits. He said, "You sold all of those suits already? That was a year's supply of inventory!"

Maybe some people just aren't cut out to be entrepreneurs. I explained to him that I was serious about helping him grow his business, and he agreed to meet with me to discuss the venture in more detail.

Later on, he came to my office, where he saw the walls adorned with many business accolades, marketing awards, and framed copies of national magazine covers that carried stories of our new products and business success. I showed him our production facility for the bicycle storage systems and shared stories about how I had not only built a multimillion-dollar business but also specialized in helping other people turn their ideas into reality. After we talked for several hours, he concluded that what he really wanted help with was getting investment capital to grow his business. He hired me to write a business and marketing plan and prepare a presentation for venture capitalists and potential investors. I wrote the plan, and within two weeks, we had generated over $150,000 in new cash capital for his business. He was happy, and while I tried to explain to him that although the new cash seemed like a lot of money, it might be just enough for him to go bankrupt. My plan called for almost double that amount, but he decided he would go forward with the plan on his own.

Fast-forward a few months. I was busy with many of my own projects and business ventures but decided to follow up to see how Floating Swimwear was doing with the new plan. I called the owner, and he was not a happy camper. He said that he was close to bankruptcy, his wife was upset with him, and his investors were angry. Confused, I said, "What happened? Did you follow the plan we laid out?" He said, "Well, not exactly. I tried something different." While I understood that he didn't want to continue to raise more capital, the $150,000 was certainly enough to increase production and grow at a steady pace. He chose a different path.

Here's where the business and marketing plans differed greatly. The plan that I had developed called for increasing the manufacturing capabilities, changing production from girls' and boys' suits to unisex suits, packaging them for distribution to pool and spa stores and mass merchants, generating free publicity for new product reviews and special interest stories, and developing new branding and a multichannel plan for different channels of distribution. This plan was developed using my research and years of experience and expertise in selling products and services that I had patented and developed. This knowledge, in combination with my many projects for other clients, gave me unique insights and a competitive edge. He decided that he had a better way, and here's what he did.

Instead of following my plan, he invested $75,000 to create infomercials to sell the swimsuits direct on late-night TV and cable. He took the other $75,000 and bought remnant commercial advertising airtime. For those of you who might not know what remnant is, it means the advertising time slots that are sold at a discount because other advertisers don't want it. Now remnant airtime advertising can work for certain types of products, but it doesn't work for the demographic that he was trying to reach to encourage them to buy floating swimwear for their children.

The reason his investors were mad, his wife was upset, and he was semisuicidal was that all the money was gone and he had sold fewer than 100 suits. You do the math: 100 swimsuits at a retail discounted price of $29 doesn't equal a positive return on investment (ROI). They say that hindsight is 20/20 vision. I can see where he was easily convinced to try that strategy, but there were too many flaws in the facilitation of the strategy.

The advertising salespeople had convinced him that he would be advertising only in demographic marketplaces that had a high capacity of pool owners and customers around water. What they didn't explain to him was that while they gave him a discount on the ad slots, those ads would be running between 2 A.M. and 4 A.M. Worse yet, instead of testing small to find out the right combination and sales conversion strategies, he opted to buy a larger advertising package to get discounts. In the end, the infomercial strategy was a financial disaster, and he asked me for more help. I explained to him that he'd spent all his money and now couldn't afford to hire Prime Concepts Group again.

Then came my blinding flash of the obvious. I asked myself, "How can we generate revenue and manage his debt, while growing the company at the same time?" The strategy of asking the right questions just seemed obvious. I think the problem with most people is that they either ask the wrong questions or they give up too soon and don't ask any questions at all.

If you're struggling with a challenge or problem, step back from the problem to get a clearer perspective, pose new questions, and allow your brain to help you come up with solutions.

It was still obvious to me that floating swimwear was a great product with great potential. The question was how we could tap that potential effectively. I offered him a deal where I would help him get his business back on track that would be mutually beneficial for both of us. The deal that I outlined for him was that we would move his business operations into our offices and production facility, and all I wanted in return was $2 commission per swimsuit sold. He could add the $2 to the cost of goods and pay me monthly on units sold for the life of the product line. He jumped at the deal, muttering that he didn't think I knew what I was doing, because how could I invest all of those resources and earn a return with only $2 per swimsuit?

Are you curious about what I did next?

I followed the original business plan. It really came down to positioning the product correctly in the marketplace. His original strategy prior to working with us was to sell them one at a time at consumer boating shows, and his next strategy was to sell at retail direct using infomercials. Both strategies created lackluster sales (and that's being generous).

His main benefit message was to save kids' lives and give parents peace of mind. That was the end result of the product, but that wasn't the benefit to the dealer market as outlined in the business plan. The benefit to dealers and chain stores was to create an instant profit center and increase sales from impulse purchases during checkout.

The obvious changes were to target the marketing message to the specific target market and to use the appropriate marketing method.

This strategy may sound simple, but it has been a foundational strategy in the success of many new product launches, new business ventures, and marketing campaigns. If you have success in your business or the company you work for, it's because you have the right combination of benefit message to a specific target market delivered using an appropriate marketing method. Even with new technologies, the Internet, social media marketing, mobile marketing, and the increased use of video marketing, that strategy still applies in every single situation, bar none.

As soon as the contract between Prime Concepts Group and Floating Swimwear was completed, we updated the marketing calendar and procured trade show space at industry trade shows. We exhibited at the National Spa & Pool Association (NSPA) trade shows on the east and west coasts, came back with more than $100,000 in sales orders, and set up hundreds of authorized Floating Swimwear dealers. Within a few short years, retail sales reached over $10 million, and Floating Swimwear, Inc., grew to 100 employees.

RECORD YOUR IDEAS!

Although this story may sound unique, stories of success like this are everywhere. Haven't you or someone you know ever seen a new product and said, "Hey, I thought of that idea years ago!" I believe that each one of us gets several great ideas each week, but unless you practice and condition yourself to write down those ideas, they will be lost just as quick as your dreams are when you wake up in the morning.

I believe the only difference between geniuses and everybody else is that geniuses capture their ideas. You don't have any excuses for not recording your own good ideas. Most likely, you have a smart phone or a phone with voice mail, and you can easily leave yourself a message, text yourself a message, or use an app to record your ideas. Do it!

JOB SECURITY DOES NOT EXIST

Another blinding flash of the obvious is that there's no such thing as job security. Job security is a myth. The only true security is in developing skills security. The more you learn, the more you can earn. The more skills you have and the more value you add, the more options you have for generating an income and creating wealth and success in the future. If you want to earn more money, then you need to add more value. There are really only two ways to gain knowledge and develop your common sense. First, you can learn the hard way, where life keeps giving you the same lesson over and over again until you learn the lesson. Second, you can learn from other people's experiences, like reading this book and the other resources in your success library. You do have a success library, don't you? If not, then this book is a great start.

Are you making life too difficult or do you have behaviors that self-sabotage your success? So far, even with the highly successful people I've had the pleasure of spending time with, I've never met anyone who couldn't benefit from new insights, experiences, and personal growth. Of course, we've all met those who think they're already perfect and don't need to learn new things. They are dangerous, and they can suck the energy right out of you because they're not open to the new ideas that the universe presents to them on a regular basis. They think they have all the answers but don't know that they don't know everything. The fear they could be wrong prevents them from admitting their mistakes or learning from their past experiences.

Live by the belief "I ask for help not because I am weak...but because I want to remain strong!"

Common sense is not so common.

— *Voltaire*

Don't find fault, find a remedy; anybody can complain.

— *Henry Ford*

42

It is the obvious which is so difficult to see most of the time. People say 'It's as plain as the nose on your face.' But how much of the nose on your face can you see, unless someone holds a mirror up to you?

—Isaac Asimov

I don't know the key to success, but the key to failure is trying to please everybody.

—Bill Cosby

Common sense is seeing things as they are; and doing things as they ought to be.

—Harriet Beecher Stowe

Action Steps to Develop the Superpower of Common Sense

1. Use your Superpower Guidebook to record your insights and perspectives on the world around you, especially your answer to "How can I add more value?"

2. Make a list of the top 10 skills you need for your career. Rate yourself on a scale of 1 to 10, with 1 being poor and 10 being excellent on how well you perform each skill set. Even if you are an expert, you can always better your best. Practice doesn't make perfect . . . practice makes improvement. Repeat the process again for the skill sets you need in all of the roles of your life, like being a parent, spouse, a friend, a colleague, a leader, or a coworker.

3. Ask yourself empowering questions on how you can improve your skill sets. You'll be amazed at how quickly your powerful brain will deliver the answers to you. This isn't a magic bullet or quick fix, but a strategy that will serve you in all areas of your life. The power of questioning is the secret asset on your journey of success.

PART 2

Where Do You Want to Go?

CHAPTER 5

Success Footprints

One of the first keys to success is leveraging the superpower of goal setting. Get clear on what you want to do, be, have, or become. Do you really know where you want to go? Whether you're reading this for improvements in your personal life or business success, it's important to have a clear destination. Do you have a clear vision? Do you know what success looks like, I mean, really looks like? If the answer is no, don't panic. I'm going to give you a few strategies and recommendations to point you in the right direction so you can get some clarity on what you want and how to achieve it. But even with a clear vision and goals, your mission is to identify, develop, and begin using your superpowers to help you get to your goals quicker and more easily than you've ever imagined. Rather than grabbing at every bright, shiny object that passes through your field of vision, set your sights on your target, and keep your focus clear.

Everyone defines success using different criteria. To be empowered, you need to buy into goals that resonate for you at a gut level. If you're trying to achieve goals set for you by other people, you most likely get short-term results. To get long-term, sustainable results, you have to get a clear outcome and understand the purpose of the goal and the specific action steps necessary to help you achieve that goal. Having learned goal setting at a young age, I just assumed that everybody understood how to set goals and achieve them. I thought there was only one basic way to set goals and achieve them, but then I started hiring employees, and I realized that people with different personalities set goals much differently. So let's take a look at the basics of goal setting and then include the little adaptations that work best for you and your dominant personality style.

One of the most common strategies for setting goals is to use the SMART goal-setting method. The first step is to capture your goals on paper, create a computer file, or download a goal-setting app to your smart phone or digital pad. (That's what your Superpower Guidebook is for.) Once you've captured your goals, compare them to the SMART criteria. It's a great place to start and a fairly simple system to learn.

SMART Goals

S = Specific

M = Measurable

A = Attainable

R = Realistic

T = Timely/Tangible

Specific: To help your mind and body achieve the goal, it needs to be specific and embedded into your unconscious. To help you get clarity, start by writing in your Superpower Guidebook exactly what you want, why you want it, and ideas and action steps on how to get there. Keep in mind that if you have a strong enough *why,* then your brain will work to give you the *how.* You'll find that you're going to want to go through the SMART criteria process at least a couple of times as you refine your goals and action plan. You will find that when you start out to set your goals, many of them may have been on your list before, but don't let that discourage you. Just because you may have failed in the past or given up on your goals does not mean that you can't begin again and achieve them.

At Prime Concepts Group, we use this process for new product launches and marketing campaigns, as well as for goals on a personal level. The SMART goals template includes these specific questions:

- What is the outcome?
- Why do we want that outcome?
- What are the benefits of accomplishing the goal?
- Is the outcome specific, and if not, how can we make it more specific?
- What does success look like?
- What criteria are we going to use to determine success?
- What do we want to accomplish?
- Who is going to be involved?
- Do we have any conflicting goals?
- What resources are at our disposal?
- Who can help us achieve the goal?
- What is the time frame and deadline?
- What are the obstacles that might get in the way of achieving the goal?
- Are there any other constraints, either internally or externally, that might hamper our progress, and if so, what is our strategy to avoid or overcome the constraints?
- Is the goal general or specific? Example: Getting in shape is a general goal, but weighing 175 pounds, being fit and flexible, and enjoying the process by a predetermined date is specific.

Measurable: Establish specific criteria for measuring your progress toward the attainment of each goal you set. When you measure your progress, it helps you stay on track and motivates you to continue the journey to reach your goals. In business, you refer to your performance and finance reports. The numbers don't lie. If you're in business or management, you know how important feedback systems are to identify problem areas and help you make course corrections. A business that operates without the proper measurements is doomed to crash and fail. Imagine your favorite sports car. Now imagine you're in that sports car blindfolded, with your foot pressed firmly on the accelerator and all of the windows in the car painted black. What do you suppose is going to happen if you can't see where you're going and you don't have any gauges? Of course, you're going to crash. As simple and as obvious as this may sound, you would be surprised how many businesses, both small and large, fail to implement and pay attention to their feedback systems and reports. For individuals with personal goals, it works the same way. You may have heard, "If you don't know where you're going, how are you going to get there?" I modify this to "If you don't know where you're going, or have measurements in place to see if you're on track, you won't reach your destination." (See the discussion on metrics later on in this book.)

Attainable: This one can be tricky. There were many times in my life when I set goals for myself that other people thought were unattainable. They would say things like I was too young or too old, not smart enough, I lacked a formal education, or didn't have adequate experience. In many cases, I proved them wrong. Over time, I developed an overwhelming belief and confidence that if I wanted something bad enough, and was willing to pay the price of the action steps, that I could reach the goal. There is a key distinction here: Are you willing to pay the price in sweat equity, persistence, risk tolerance, and the possibility of failure? Of course, we don't aim to fail, but if you fail to plan, you'll certainly fail or at least not reach your potential success. So the *attainable* criterion in this case relates more to your belief system than to whether the goal is really attainable. At the time of writing this book, I am a national director and board member of the National Speakers Association (NSA). For more than 17 years, I've been a member in this organization filled with thought leaders, professional speakers, authors, trainers, and consultants on every topic imaginable, both business and personal.

There are thousands of stories of individuals who overcame huge obstacles, both physically and mentally, to achieve amazing results. Stories of success and achievement range from overcoming disease and physical handicaps that offer inspiration to the masses, to building multimillion-dollar corporations and countless foundations and charities. One of the reasons that organizations and corporations hire professional speakers is to help their team members increase their performance and results.

As a business growth expert, I'm hired to transform their leadership and staff to use their resources, along with my unique strategies of business and marketing success. Many times, I'm a third-party endorsement for the executive team for what they know is possible. They just lack the strategies to get there. I help connect the dots between a company's value proposition and their target marketplace to help them find, attract, and keep their customers. So what I think is attainable, what you think is attainable, and what other people think is attainable are likely to be very different. Your challenge is to develop the attitudes, skills, and abilities, along with the financial capacity, to reach your goals. Like anything else, the more you do it, the better you become.

Realistic: My first question here is "What does *realistic* mean to you?" This criterion is similar to *attainable* in that it's more a state of mind than whether it's achievable. Realistic doesn't mean easy. Realistic, in the SMART goal-setting system, means doable. It means that you believe you can do it, that the skills needed are available, and, on a business level, that the goal fits the overall vision of the company. Years ago, I had the pleasure of being the business manager for one of the world's most popular motivational speakers, Les Brown. I helped him capture many new opportunities, develop new products, get more speaking engagements, increase attendance at his live events, and triple his business in the first six months. Les Brown, like me, came from meager beginnings and poor neighborhoods and lived in the projects. He used to say, "Aim for the moon, because even if you miss, you still land among the stars." Now the question of what's realistic is important, but make sure you're not allowing limiting beliefs to set your expectations too low.

For example, I'm over 50 years old now and have never played basketball on a team of any level in my life, so it's unlikely, and not realistic, for me to think that I'm going to play NBA basketball. Nor is it realistic to think that if I aim and run east that I'll ever see a sunset, as I would be going in the wrong direction.

This criterion is important because each time you set a goal and miss the mark, you can lower your self-esteem. If you lower your self-esteem too much, you give up or fail to try at all. As you refer back to your goals list, ask yourself if you truly believe that your goal is realistic, and if not, why not? What would you have to do, have, or become to make your goal more realistic? Can you become the type of person who has the attitude, aptitude, discipline, and consistency to reach your goal? This is where having an unrealistic expectation or conflicting goal sets you up for potential failure.

If you love chocolate and fast food, overeat, don't exercise, and have a goal to lose weight, then how can you expect your goal of losing weight to be realistic? The reality is that it's not realistic — unless, of course, you're willing to change your mind-set and behavior, which is entirely possible (and what this book is about) for each and every one of us. You just need to get enough leverage and the proper strategy to replace the old behaviors with new behaviors.

Timely/Tangible: Your goals need a deadline. Without a deadline, there's no sense of urgency. A deadline for your goal helps your unconscious mind influence your decisions and action steps to reach your goal. Set dates for short-term goals and long-term goals. If the goal or project is large, intermediate dates and milestones along the way help keep you on track. At Prime Concepts Group, we use an online project management tracking system called BaseCampHQ that allows all of our staff members and clients to see the timelines, phases, and milestones for their projects.

Specific timelines, benchmarks, and deadlines are critical to success and goal setting. In the 1980s, I was a speed skater who competed nationally, and I later became a professional cyclist.

(Don't get too excited; I was only a category three USCF cyclist, and pros like Greg LeMond and Lance Armstrong were category one professional cyclists.) Having training and racing goals, both short-term and long-term, were critical components the coaching staff used to motivate, inspire, and improve us. Now I just ride recreationally, but I still rely on my Garmin GPS cycling computer to measure my performance and improve. It even has a virtual trainer to pace your speed and performance, and after the ride, you can review a wide variety of statistics online. Using a tracking method to measure performance can help you forecast future results. When in the goal-setting process, you use limiting language like "someday" or "maybe," you're setting yourself up for failure.

The key point is to get absolute clarity and certainty on why and when you're going to achieve your goals. And remember, the *why* is more important than the *how*. The tangible part of this criterion means that you can experience it with one or more of your senses, meaning you can taste it, touch it, see it, hear it, or feel it. When your goal has a tangible component, you have a much better chance of attaining it. Now get going!

Goals are the fuel in the furnace of achievement.

—Brian Tracy

In absence of clearly defined goals, we become strangely loyal to performing daily acts of trivia.

—Author Unknown

I honestly think it is better to be a failure at something you love than to be a success at something you hate.

—George Burns

I've failed over and over and over again in my life and that is why I succeed.

—Michael Jordan

Goals. There's no telling what you can do when you get inspired by them. There's no telling what you can do when you believe in them. There's no telling what will happen when you act upon them.

—*Jim Rohn*

Aim for the top. There is plenty of room there. There are so few at the top it is almost lonely there.

—*Samuel Insull*

The goal you set must be challenging. At the same time, it should be realistic and attainable, not impossible to reach. It should be challenging enough to make you stretch, but not so far that you break.

—*Rick Hansen*

You must have long term goals to keep you from being frustrated by short term failures.

—*Charles C. Noble*

What you get by achieving your goals is not as important as what you become by achieving your goals.

—*Zig Ziglar*

First say to yourself what you would be; and then do what you have to do.

—*Epictetus*

The person with a fixed goal, a clear picture of his desire, or an ideal always before him, causes it, through repetition, to be buried deeply in his subconscious mind and is thus enabled, thanks to its generative and sustaining power, to realize his goal in a minimum of time and with a minimum of physical effort. Just pursue the thought unceasingly. Step by step you will achieve realization, for all your faculties and powers become directed to that end.

—*Claude M. Bristol*

Goal-Setting Action Steps

1. Perform a brain dump of all the goals you want to achieve, both short-term (this month or year) and long-term (next three to five years and beyond).

2. Chunk them into specific categories, for example, personal, professional, relationships, wealth, and health.

3. Write out 10 reasons why you have to achieve the goal and why you must achieve the goal this time.

4. Write out everything you have to gain and everything you have to lose by not attaining the goal to ensure that you have the proper leverage and motivation to reach the goal.

5. Once you have clarity on your reasons, then go through the SMART goal-setting system.

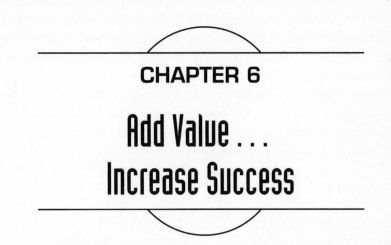

CHAPTER 6

Add Value...
Increase Success

The strategy of adding more value to increase your success relates to many areas of your life, so whether you are unemployed, a student, a work-at-home parent, an executive, or part of a team, you can benefit from asking yourself, "How can I add more value?"

In an earlier chapter, I asked you to identify the skill sets necessary for success in the different roles of your life, like being a parent, a spouse, a friend, a colleague, a leader, and a coworker. Did you do the exercise? If not, now would be a good time to complete it. Looking back on your observations, how did you do? By rating yourself on a scale of 1 to 10, you can identify areas and find gaps for improvement. Once you have the list, you can develop a strategy and define the action steps for personal growth and development.

One of my friends and colleagues, Roxanne Emmerich, has a favorite saying: "Life gives to the givers...and takes from the takers!" Although it's obvious that bad things sometimes happen to good people, the point is that the more you give, the more that comes back to you in positive ways.

A great example of a giver who plays many different roles in my life is business mogul and philanthropist Dr. Nido Qubein. He came to the United States as a teenager with little knowledge of English, no contacts, and only $50 in his pocket. His life has been an amazing success story. As an educator, he is president of High Point University, an undergraduate and graduate institution with 4,500 students from 51 countries. He has authored two dozen books and audio programs distributed worldwide. His foundation provides scholarships to 48 deserving young people each year. To date, the Qubein Foundation has granted more than 700 scholarships, worth over $6 million. As a business leader, he is chairman of Great Harvest Bread Company, with 220 stores, and he serves on the boards of national organizations such as BB&T (a Fortune 500 company with $164 billion in assets), the La-Z-Boy Corporation (one of the largest and most recognized furniture brands worldwide), and Dots Stores (a chain of fashion boutiques with more than 400 locations across the country).

Nido Qubein is the youngest person ever inducted in the International Speaker Hall of Fame, and he is the founder of the prestigious National Speakers Foundation in Phoenix, Arizona. If that isn't enough to convince you of his credentials, consider that he has been the recipient of many honors, including the Ellis Island Medal of Honor, the Horatio Alger Award for Distinguished Americans, the Order of the Long Leaf Pine (North Carolina's highest civic award), a Doctorate of Laws degree, Sales and Marketing International's Ambassador of Free Enterprise, induction into the Global Society for Outstanding Business Leadership, and Citizen of the Year and Philanthropist of the Year in his home city of High Point, North Carolina.

I've considered him a mentor long before I ever met him personally, from listening to his CDs and attending his live presentations. Over the years, our paths have crossed many times, and now I've been able to see firsthand how his attitude of giving and adding more value has contributed to his many successes. Nido invited me to tour the campus of High Point University and work with his leadership team on their branding and marketing strategies. While I was honored that he asked me for my observations and ideas, a small part of me was thinking, "He's already got it all figured out. Why does he need my help?" Nido understands that you can learn from everyone and every situation, and he was able to tap into my unique insights. He credits his success to his insatiable desire for improvement and his giving spirit. I was at High Point for two days, and when leaving, I was presented with many gifts of appreciation — so many, in fact, that I had to ship them back to my office because they wouldn't fit in my luggage. Over the following months, I received more thank-you cards, books, interesting articles, and other gifts!

You can learn more about Nido, his remarkable personal story, and his valuable resources at www.nidoqubein.com and at www .highpoint.edu/president.php and en.wikipedia.org/wiki/Nido_ Qubein.

ADD VALUE, MAKE A PROFIT

At my company, Prime Concepts Group, LLC, our core mission of helping our clients prosper is to add value, make a profit. This concept just makes good business sense: The more value you add, the larger profits you will receive, the more success you will achieve. Although the term *generating profits* has been given a bad rap in the media from companies that abused their customers' and shareholders' trust, the measurement of success in business definitely has a financial component. If a business doesn't generate a profit, then it won't be in business very long . . . at least in a free market economy.

When you add more value, customers buy more frequently, and in larger quantities, and tell more of their friends about the fantastic benefits of your products and services. We alluded to this elsewhere when we talked about how to increase your earn ability by increasing your learn ability. It's so important that it is worth a deeper look.

During the recent recession, when many businesses failed or downsized, we were able to grow and help other businesses grow, while having record-setting years. One of the factors of our success is that we want to keep things as simple as possible. As I've mentioned, simple doesn't always mean easy, but I think many organizations have too much waste in unrefined or overcomplicated processes, inadequately trained staff, or consistent branding and marketing efforts.

Adding more value is what sets my soul on fire. It's what gets me excited and makes me want to jump out of bed every day. The joy and rewards that come from this type of focus allow me to tap into innovation and creativity and provide an almost unlimited feeling of energy. Tapping into my innovation superpower allows me to solve problems and give birth to new ideas. It's the foundation for developing business growth strategies, improving team performance, inventing new product and service offerings, and transforming business revenues.

Imagine how implementing the concept of adding more value can affect your life and the lives of those around you. Consumers are more informed and have instant access to websites that allow customer reviews, product ratings, and price comparisons, and by adding more value, you'll gain a competitive edge, capture market share, and grow your business. If you are in business or responsible for helping to generate sales, then creating compelling value propositions and communicating them effectively should be a primary goal. Adding value translates into solving problems and delivering an implied state-of-mind feeling and benefits. If you're in leadership or management of an organization, then defining and communicating your company's mission, vision, and objectives helps you attract and retain top talent. It's wise to develop and implement a plan for communicating how you add more value throughout your website, social media, and all your traditional marketing methods

This philosophy can carry over into every aspect of your personal and professional life.

Knowing the value you have to offer is a superpower. Learning how to clearly state what that value is, so that clients and potential customers can make good buying decisions, will help you achieve success and boost sales. Knowing what that value is for your personal goals will make all the difference . . . if you're motivated to take action.

Until you value yourself, you won't value your time. Until you value your time, you will not do anything with it.

—*M. Scott Peck*

You can have everything in life that you want if you just give enough other people what they want.

—*Zig Ziglar*

Doing well is the result of doing good. That's what capitalism is all about.

—*Ralph Waldo Emerson*

Unemployment is capitalism's way of getting you to plant a garden.

—*Orson Scott Card*

Americans chose a free enterprise system designed to provide a quality of opportunity, not compel a quality of results. And that is why this is the only place in the world where you can open up a business in the spare bedroom of your home.

—*Marco Rubio*

Any one who believes that any great enterprise of an industrial character can be started without labor must have little experience of life.

—*William Graham Sumner*

Price is what you pay. Value is what you get.

—*Warren Buffett*

What we must decide is perhaps how we are valuable, rather than how valuable we are.

—*Edgar Z. Friedenberg*

What we obtain too cheap, we esteem too lightly.

—*Thomas Paine*

We know the true worth of a thing when we have lost it.

—*French Proverb*

If you don't set a baseline standard for what you'll accept in life, you'll find it's easy to slip into behaviors and attitudes or a quality of life that's far below what you deserve.

—Anthony Robbins

We get paid for bringing value to the market place.

—Jim Rohn

Carry on any enterprise as if all future success depended on it.

—Cardinal Richelieu

AN EXERCISE TO DEVELOP AND INCREASE YOUR VALUE

Pick one goal you want to focus on. Identify at least 20 positive benefits (value) of this goal to your customers and 20 positive benefits (value) that will result for you or your business.

- If this is a personal goal, what is the value that you will receive personally by completing this goal? What is the value that others will receive when you achieve your goal?
- If this is a business growth goal, what is the value to your customers (benefits they will receive) from utilizing your services or purchasing your product? And in return for offering your customers this great value, what is the resulting value offered to the growth of your organization.

Now compare the two lists you just created for value. If the value list is longer for the benefits *you* will receive than the list for your customers, do not expect to be successful or enjoy profitable sales. You're going to have to increase the value, or perceived value, to your customers for them to buy from your business. Let's keep thinking about how we're going to make that happen.

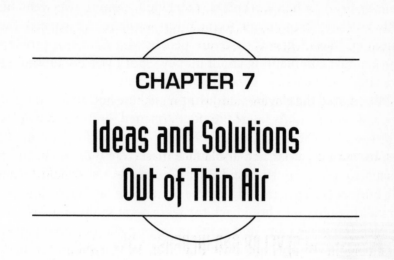

CHAPTER 7

Ideas and Solutions
Out of Thin Air

There is no such thing as a money problem; there is only a lack of ideas.

If you want to earn more money, then come up with more ideas. If money can fix it, it's not a problem. There's no shortage of money in the world; you just have to find a way to be more innovative to add the value that creates the exchange of currency. I realize that these concepts may seem very foreign to you, and that some people may even be a bit angry about my perspective. So before youre inclined to send an e-mail or letter trying to prove me wrong and explaining to me all the reasons that the economy, your education, your family, your environment, or your circumstances have kept you back, I'd like you to consider the following true story, which may help you to approach this section of the book with an open mind.

Many years ago, early on in my career, I came home from working on one of my business ventures. I was frustrated from lack of cash flow, and my business wasn't growing as fast as I thought it should be growing. The woman I was dating at the time got tired of me complaining about my problems and said, "You don't have any problems, so why don't you focus on the solutions." Now we'd only been dating for a couple weeks, and I knew she was a nurse but

I never been to her workplace. Later that evening, we went on a little journey. She took me to the hospital where she worked. I was thinking, "Yes, I know, there are people who have real problems, and I'm just complaining about money." But I was not emotionally prepared for the lesson I was about to receive.

We entered the elevator, and she pressed the button for the fourth floor. A few seconds later, the doors opened, and we walked into a little room where we had to wash our hands and put on medical scrubs, booties, a hairnet, and a face mask. We walked around the corner to a hallway that said Burn Center. As we walked through the burn center, she introduced me to many of her burn patients. It was all I could do to hold back the tears because these people were in such immense pain, and many of them could not even use pain medicine. It was an experience that I'll never forget, and it made a profound impact on my belief system.

When companies select me for a keynote presentation, the meeting planners are sent a preprogram questionnaire. One of the questions I always ask is "What are the top three goals you have for my program?" Because I am selected for business growth-related topics, their program goals include helping their leadership and teams be more innovative and creative. They want their attendees to leave the presentation with fresh new ideas that help them improve performance and results. They want to leverage all of their marketing and sales efforts to connect to the marketplace, engage their customers, and gain a competitive edge.

So whether it's expanding someone's digital footprint on the Internet, increasing targeted traffic to their website, or using new forms of marketing, like video sales letters, mobile, and geolocation promotions, it comes down to being innovative and creative. I've been a student of innovation and creativity for my entire life and a serial entrepreneur who's generated millions of dollars in sales from ideas. I guess you'd say—generating ideas out of thin air.

You don't have to be an entrepreneur, or even be employed, to benefit from unleashing your innovation talents and learning new creativity techniques.

INNOVATION AND CREATIVITY

Innovation and creativity are two big superpowers, and unfortunately, they seem to get schooled out of many people. Creative people aren't necessarily the best educated and don't have the highest IQs. In fact, because of the way the formal education system is designed, it often squelches creativity. Much of what is taught in the school system is simply memorization, which inhibits creativity. And the way math and sciences are often taught also focuses only on the logical side, to the detriment of creative thinking. We take beautiful, bright six-year-olds—full of creativity—and tell them to sit up straight at their desks, not talk, and raise their hand when they want to go to the bathroom. Eventually, the school system beats their creativity into submission.

In fact, recent research in the fields of perception, psychobiology, and neuroscience have revealed that there is more than one area of intelligence. They have discovered at least six—each one hardwired into a different area of the brain. The people we consider geniuses (like Mozart and Einstein) have succeeded in tapping into a second area of intelligence, or possibly a third. Nearly everyone else works in mostly one region of the brain and uses less than 10 percent of their brain's capacity.

So why aren't most people more creative? Well, there are several reasons. Most people don't need to be creative for most of the areas of their lives. Think about it. You probably have many routines that you haven't changed for a long time: what time you get up in the morning, the route you drive to work, your daily routines, the food you eat, the restaurants you frequent, the people you hang out with, or the shows you watch on TV. Our mental conditioning has formed our beliefs, behaviors, actions, effects, and results. There is certainly a purpose for these routines, and without them, our lives would be in chaos, but when it comes to idea generation, innovation, and creativity, you have to be willing to shake things up a little. You have to be ready to change your mental channel, and I'll share several strategies for doing that in just a moment.

Creative People Are

- Curious about the world
- Self-motivated
- Avid readers
- Independent
- Delighted by novelty
- Risk takers
- Deeply involved in their work
- World travelers

These characteristics provide creative people with a very rich diet of stimulation, variety, and situations. They are exposed to a steady stream of new opinions, languages, cultures, and attitudes. They see a much broader spectrum of society, people in general, and the world. They see the same thing handled in many different ways, so it opens up their minds to problem solving, lateral thinking, and innovation.

See whether you can read the following paragraph:

Aoccdrnig to rscheearch at Cmabrigde Uinervtisy, it deosn't mttaer in waht oredr the ltteers occur in a word. The olny iprmoatnt tihng is taht the frist and lsat ltteer be at the rghit pclae. The rset can be a total mses and you can sitll raed it wouthit porbelm. Tihs is bcuseae the huamn mnid deos not raed ervey lteter by istlef, but the wrod as a wlohe. Amzanig, huh?

You were able to understand and read it because you've been conditioned through repetition by reading the English language. Many of us have been conditioned to think that the best ideas are in someone else's head. And probably the biggest culprit that stops or limits creativity is the limiting belief of saying to yourself, "I'm just not creative."

As you can imagine, if you believe you're not creative, you probably won't take much action to change that, unless you're properly motivated. It's difficult to be creative if you're always following the rules, afraid to make mistakes, or focused on the right answer. Certainly, there are times when there is only one answer, but if you think there's only one answer, then you will stop looking as soon as you find one. The world is full of possibilities. Your world is filled with possibilities and with a belief like that, you can become unstoppable.

With my street-smart education, I learned from necessity to be innovative and creative to survive and thrive. I'm certain that most of the people reading this book have much more formal education than I do. But formal education is not a guarantee of creativity and innovation! If you want to think, act, and perform with less effort and better results, then becoming more innovative and creative will help you.

Do you need to have your back up against a wall to see a creative solution? I don't think so, but you do need the ability to see a multitude of possible scenarios to choose from before making a final decision.

Do you ever watch movies at home on DVD? A lot of them give you extra footage to watch, and sometimes you get a chance to see footage that didn't make it into the final cut of the movie and at least one or two endings that they filmed but didn't choose to use for the film. Sometimes when I watch these alternative endings, I agree with the one they chose, but other times I like one of the unused endings better. But I would have never known without seeing all three versions to choose from.

When you have a problem, do you use your creative superpowers to come up with at least two or three different ideas and solutions for your issue? Can you view the movie in your head to play different scenarios of what would happen for each of them, so you can confidently pick the idea and solution that your common sense tells you will be best for the given situation? And have you filed the unused solutions in a safe place, in the event that you need to edit what you've done and utilize one of your other scenarios?

> Creativity means being ready, willing, and able to see things differently.
>
> When everyone in the room is thinking alike, then no one is thinking creatively.
>
> When two people in business always agree, then one of them is unnecessary.

YOUR CREATIVITY QUOTIENT

My good friend and business partner, Randy Gage, is one of my creativity buddies. Lord knows we certainly haven't agreed on everything over the years, but our experiences, our integrative eyes, and our ability to see the world from many perspectives make for a great team. With his permission, I would like to share the following quiz, which he created for measuring the Creativity Quotient.

What's Your Creativity Quotient?

1. Do you fail a lot, because you are willing to try many new high-risk endeavors?

   ☐ YES   ☐ NO

2. Are you highly self-motivated?

   ☐ YES   ☐ NO

3. Do you have vivid, colorful dreams, many of which you remember in the morning?

   ☐ YES   ☐ NO

4. Do you enjoy learning about other cultures and nationalities and exploring other languages and customs?

   ☐ YES   ☐ NO

5. Have you traveled internationally and extensively?

☐ YES   ☐ NO

6. Do you ask a lot of what-if questions that challenge current accepted norms?

☐ YES   ☐ NO

7. Do you hear a song for the first time, or the start of a sentence, and know how it will finish? Or likewise, do you know the outcome of a TV show or movie, five minutes into it?

☐ YES   ☐ NO

8. Are you more emotional than most people?

☐ YES   ☐ NO

9. Do you have a career that involves writing, acting, painting, singing, or other artistic endeavors?

☐ YES   ☐ NO

10. Are you the kind of person who isn't happy and productive unless you're doing at least four or five tasks simultaneously?

☐ YES   ☐ NO

11. Do people tell you that you're a clotheshorse or dress stylishly?

☐ YES   ☐ NO

12. Do you look at a situation and see how things could be better arranged to work better?

☐ YES   ☐ NO

13. Did you excel in creative writing or drama when you were in school?

☐ YES   ☐ NO

14. Do you come up with a steady stream of original ideas in response to what happens to you each day?

☐ YES   ☐ NO

15. Do you adapt easily to a new job, home, or school?

☐ YES   ☐ NO

16. Do you daydream a lot, picturing yourself in different scenarios?

   ☐ YES   ☐ NO

17. Do you often get struck with a flash of insight when you've left a problem to percolate in your subconscious mind?

   ☐ YES   ☐ NO

18. Do you usually read four or five books at a time?

   ☐ YES   ☐ NO

19. Do you take disengagement breaks from a creative project that you are momentarily stuck on?

   ☐ YES   ☐ NO

20. Have you made a sharp change in lifestyle preference—such as going from a conservative dresser to a funky one, antique furniture to contemporary, metal rock to opera—since becoming an adult?

   ☐ YES   ☐ NO

Use the Following Table for Scoring Instructions:

Add up the number of times you answered YES. Keep in mind that this little quiz is meant to measure only ONE area of your genius. You could score zero on it but still be a bona fide genius in other areas. In fact, many people who have two or three college degrees will score very low. That's because the education process has subjugated their creativity.

The point of this test is to determine where you are exactly in the creativity sector only. I believe that you can develop your genius in all areas. So even if you feel like creativity is not one of your strengths—it can be learned. We just need to know your starting point. With that in mind, here's how I would categorize the scores:

0–5 You are below even the creativity levels of the masses. You may be highly educated or just someone who is very strong in logical, analytical processes. You are missing a great deal in life because you haven't let your creative kid come out to play in a long time.

Doing so will open a whole new universe in your problem-solving and innovation abilities.

6–10 You are about average in creativity, which is a polite way to say mediocre. You are certainly on a level with the rest of society, but that's no place to stake out a comfort zone.

11–15 You are above average in your creative skills. That's always a good place to be, but there is still room at the top, particularly if you scored 11 or 12. A small improvement from this level makes for significant rewards, both personally and professionally.

16–20 If you scored 16 or higher, this is where the cool kids with the pumped-up kicks live. You're in the creative genius category.

So how did you score, and what do you think of the quiz? Record your thoughts in your Superpower Guidebook.

Now that you know you need to put yourself in the proper mindset, let's explore a few of the tools that will help you become more innovative and creative.

Here are a few techniques you can use to get your creative juices flowing.

Cross-Train Your Brain

- Drive a different route to work.
- Move your watch, ring, or wallet to a new place for a week.
- Sit in a new place for meetings and meals.
- Strike up a conversation with someone you don't know or would normally avoid.
- Change sides of the bed.
- Use your nondominant hand to eat, brush your teeth, and make phone calls.
- Get some creativity toys for your desk area.
- Identify all the geometric shapes you can see from wherever you are now.

- Find solitude.
- Listen to a different style of music.
- Create an idea-friendly environment.

CAPTURE YOUR THOUGHTS

We alluded to the concept of journaling in previous chapters, but as it relates to creativity, I have to repeat that having a separate place to capture and record your ideas is a sign of genius. I keep a notebook near my bed, travel with my iPad, and usually have my iPhone with me so I can capture my ideas on paper or with audio applications. Another helpful option I've used in the past is to call my voice mail and leave myself a message with the idea. Use your Superpower Guidebook! It can go by any number of other names, of course:

- Brilliant Idea Journal
- Project Journal
- Life Journal
- Idea Capture File

BRAINSTORMING

I like to refer to brainstorming as idea storming. One of the ways to find a good idea is to generate lots of ideas. There are many synergistic benefits to brainstorming in a small group. Here are a few tips to make your brainstorming sessions most effective: Set a time limit. I recommend no more than 15- to 20-minute sessions, or even shorter. Assign a neutral facilitator. If you're the CEO or manager, select one of your team members to be the facilitator. Remember, no criticism during brainstorming. If someone tosses out idea and you say, "Hey, that's great!" or "No, that won't work," then you are going to limit the flow of ideas. Think wacky, and go for quantity versus quality. Practice piggybacking on previous ideas.

If your group is reluctant to openly share their ideas in public, then you can distribute Post-it notepads or index cards—all the same color, or it defeats the purpose—or have them prepare their ideas in writing prior to the session. This allows the individual to remain anonymous. Once you've gathered several ideas, the next step is to clarify, discuss, categorize, eliminate items, and prioritize your list. Keep the brainstorming session fun and fast, and summarize your action steps.

IDEA MAPPING AND MIND MAPPING

One of the all-time greatest techniques for getting creative juices flowing and really thinking off the chain is mind mapping. This is a process that is inherently creative by its nature. Instead of thinking laterally, which is the way most people approach an idea, you are exploring the idea and expanding it in many different directions without a logical pattern. This allows you to come up with new and fresh perspectives that you couldn't otherwise. Mind mapping is an integral part of our business operations. We use it during consultations, in planning marketing campaigns, for capturing ideas from brainstorming sessions, in developing workflow processes and website design structure, and for training and development. Mind mapping is an accelerated learning technique that allows you to learn faster, recall information quicker, and retain content longer. I create mind maps when I am reading books, listening to audio programs, and doing every other type of knowledge consumption.

The mind maps allow me to work more visually and are less restrictive. This is not to say that the traditional concept of creating an outline is not effective. They are just different techniques with different purposes. We start with the mind map and then, if necessary, move it to an outline format. Mind mapping is a concept that was coined by Tony Buzan many years ago and has been adapted by different people throughout the years. I used to do all my mind maps on paper, but now I prefer mind-mapping software. The software I use is from a company named Mind Jet. You can get a trial of the software at www.mindjet.com. There are also smart phone, iPhone, and Android phone apps and digital pad apps from various companies. Use your favorite search engine or application store.

Here are some suggestions for mind mapping:

- Start with a blank piece of paper, preferably one without lines. I start by making a circle in the center of the page with the main topic or focus.
- Use association — Use lines, arrows, colors, and codes to indicate relationships and connections between ideas.
- Use emphasis — Start with a central image or word to focus the eye and brain, and trigger associations. Use images, colors, dimension, and size to reflect relative importance.
- Be clear — Print key words, with only one word on a line.
- Leave space — Allow yourself room to add new branches and subtopics.
- Create your own style — These are guidelines, not rules. Discover what works best for you.
- As you read the rest of this book, create a mind map to capture your ideas and action steps.

THE SCAMPER TECHNIQUE

This was first developed by Bob Eberle and Alex Osborne to develop more creativity in the workplace. It's a helpful technique for viewing solutions to a challenge. SCAMPER is an acronym for seven different ways you can view an idea. This process may seem silly or crazy, but it's the kind of technique that lets bold, daring, and imaginative ideas come forth.

Remember, creativity is like a muscle; it can be strengthened with exercise.

S–Substitute

C–Combine

A–Adapt

M–Modify

P–Put to other uses

E–Eliminate

R–Reverse/Rearrange

An example of SCAMPER using an umbrella:

Substitute: Use a plastic bag stretched over a wire coat hanger.

Combine: Add a radio and digital clock to the handle.

Adapt: Make it useful for joggers by attaching it to the body.

Modify: Make it big enough to cover several people at once.

Put to other uses: Use the tip for poking holes or picking up scrap paper.

Eliminate: Take away the metal spokes that are always bending.

Reverse: Have the umbrella fold up instead of down to catch the water.

I've mentioned already that all creative geniuses have some method for capturing and internalizing experiences. Just having varied experiences is not enough. You must capture them, so you can receive nourishment from them.

QUESTIONING

A great way to stimulate creative thinking is asking questions. The kinds of questions you want to ask are what-if and possibility questions like:

- But if it was possible, how could it be done?
- In what ways might I (we) attract new customers?

- In what ways might I become more creative?
- What if we started over from ground zero and did it another way?

ANOTHER USEFUL TECHNIQUE: USE ANALOGY THINKING

Analogy thinking is taking an existing situation and applying it in a totally different context. For example, I once took the concept of a radio commercial promoting a radio station and applied it in a display ad for a local restaurant. Often you can take a practice that is used in one business and apply it to another industry or business. Looking at what happens in totally unrelated situations can often provide brilliant insight and inspiration about the situation you are working on. Make an analogy to another business or situation, look at their solutions, and then discover new ideas about your own situation.

CHILDLIKE PERSPECTIVE

One of the best and most creative ways to approach any situation needing innovation or creativity is to think like a five-year-old. That is the point in most people's lives when they are at their peak creative state, before it's drummed out of them. Children at that age don't concern themselves with government regulations, social etiquette, or accepted practices. They just focus on what they want to accomplish and how that can be done. They have a sense of wonder about the entire world. Elevators are magic. Escalators are simply amazing. And airplanes are a thing of beauty.

AN ATTITUDE OF WONDER

Tap into your Wonder Quotient. When was the last time you spent a day being truly amazed by most of what you encountered? Yes, the Panama Canal, the Great Wall of China, and the Pyramids are breathtaking. But do you have a clue how astounding a can opener is? Do you have any idea how amazing it is that a 747 can fly in the air? Do you realize how astonishing elevators are? Visit a museum, library, or theme park. Look for the wonder everywhere. We have one room in our house that's dedicated to creativity. It's a favorite place for my wife and me because it's filled with painting canvases, musical instruments, and a variety of craft projects. You're not going to see my art projects in any gallery soon, but my wife, Aliesa, is becoming quite the artist in her own right. Spending time with her has helped me view the world with an attitude of wonder and amazement.

ESCAPISM

Propose the wildest, most outrageous, most preposterous things you can imagine. They do not have to be practical, possible, or even sensible. You use true escapism where there are no morals, rules, etiquette, laws, or standards. You escape the physical limitations of the world to see what your ultimate solution would be.

Once you have done this, and only when you have finished, should you look back at the ideas you have generated. Then you should look for ways in which all or part of these ideas could be made practical. Think of the benefits you could gain by using the idea, and work out how you can achieve the same thing in reality. How could you modify the suggested solution to make it work? What changes in the world would you need to make the idea possible, and how can you make those changes happen?

Let's summarize some important creativity concepts:

- Everyone, you included, is naturally creative and not subject to any required personality or intelligence limitations.
- Your creative spirit grows by using your curiosity.
- You can tap into your creativity by expanding your comfort zone.

- Make creative thinking and idea generation a separate process from evaluation.
- Identify and check your premises about a problem or situation.
- Create an idea-friendly environment.
- Break away from your customary ways of thinking about a problem or issue.
- Adopt new, unique, and different perspectives on a situation.
- Remove creativity blocks and negative thinking; think in possibilities.

The human mind, once stretched to a new idea, never goes back to its original dimensions.

— *Oliver Wendell Holmes*

Imagination is more important than knowledge.

— *Albert Einstein*

You see things; and you say, 'Why?' But I dream things that never were; and I say, 'Why not?'

— *George Bernard Shaw*

The key question isn't 'What fosters creativity?' But it is why in God's name isn't everyone creative? Where was the human potential lost? How was it crippled? I think therefore a good question might be not why do people create? But why do people not create or innovate? We have got to abandon that sense of amazement in the face of creativity, as if it were a miracle if anybody created anything.

— *Abraham Maslow*

Nothing is done. Everything in the world remains to be done or done over. The greatest picture is not yet painted, the greatest play isn't written, the greatest poem is unsung. There isn't in all the world a perfect railroad, nor a good government, nor a sound law. Physics, mathematics, and especially the most advanced and exact of the sciences are being fundamentally revised.... Psychology, economics, and sociology are awaiting a Darwin, whose work in turn is awaiting an Einstein.

—Lincoln Steffens

The world is but a canvas to the imagination.

—Henry David Thoreau

We have come to think of art and work as incompatible, or at least independent categories and have for the first time in history created an industry without art.

—Ananda K. Coomaraswamy

Creativity is . . . seeing something that doesn't exist already. You need to find out how you can bring it into being and that way be a playmate with God.

—Michele Shea

The most potent muse of all is our own inner child.

—Stephen Nachmanovitch

As competition intensifies, the need for creative thinking increases. It is no longer enough to do the same thing better . . . no longer enough to be efficient and solve problems.

—Edward de Bono

We don't stop playing because we grow old; we grow old because we stop playing.

—George Bernard Shaw

Action Steps for Developing Your Innovation and Creativity Superpowers

1. Select your favorite method for capturing your ideas and start today.

2. Integrate mind mapping in your personal and professional lives.

3. Cross-train yourself by getting out of your comfort zone and experiencing new things, places, and people.

CHAPTER 8

Critical Thinking Tactics

Are you ready to put on your critical thinking cap?

Critical thinking is a superpower. It's different from the thinking most people do. When you make decisions, are you taking some kind of constructive action or simply reacting to the current situation? If your answer is action, then congratulations; you're using your critical thinking superpower to help you make good decisions. If your normal mode of response is to react, you may spend your time feeling like you're spinning out of control, making poor, fear-based decisions, and you may be living your life in survival mode rather than success mode.

In the 1980s, I was an in-line speed skater who competed in national competitions. One of the benefits was the opportunity to train at the Olympic Training Center in Colorado Springs, Colorado. I was lucky enough to train there two different times, and it was a wonderful experience. Although I never competed in the Olympics, just training like an Olympian was an amazing feeling. Back then, I weighed 168 pounds and was strong, fit, and flexible. I was burning so many calories each week that I could pretty much eat whatever I wanted. After speed skating for years, I took up road cycling, first recreationally and then as a USCF-licensed bicycle racer. It was an easy transition from speed skating to cycling because I was using the same muscle groups.

In road cycling, there are five categories of licensed racers. I raced in category three (CAT3) out of five. To give us perspective, Lance Armstrong was a category one (CAT1 Pro) cyclist. I was fast, but I certainly didn't put in the time and dedication to move up. After bicycle racing for a couple of years and then inventing the PedaStyle® bicycle storage system and building up my sporting goods company, first racing and then working out took a backseat in my life. There certainly wasn't any critical thought in the decision. Life just took over, or I let it.

Fast-forward to 10 years later. I had ballooned from 168 pounds to 268, in what seemed like only a blink of an eye. So how could a former Olympic-caliber athlete turn himself into a clinically obese, financially indebted, unhappily married, struggling entrepreneur? Well, for starters, I'd given up on my superpowers and allowed my belief system to accept a fear-based lack mentality.

Sure, I could blame the fact that I stopped cycling on my first wife's complaints about how much time I was spending on my bicycle. Or I could blame the economy for increased aluminum prices at a time when I had a contract to sell my products to Wal-Mart that caused me to lose several hundred thousand dollars. Or I could blame the fact that I was an orphan who grew up with few role models and in the name of discipline was physically abused by foster parents who beat me with a belt to the point of hospitalization, making *discipline* a dirty word for me. Or I could blame the weight gain on getting older or fast-food companies. Or I could blame the fact that I never learned how to cook for myself and ate 90 percent of my meals at fast-food restaurants. All those and a host of other excuses are just that—excuses.

It would be easy to blame everybody else for that period of my life, but as a critical thinker and student of prosperity consciousness, I recognize that I was responsible for all those choices, just as I am responsible for all the decisions I make on a daily basis. I am responsible for all the choices I've made along this journey, and I'm in control of my own destiny. My desire in writing this book is to pay it forward. The proverbial *it* refers to the lessons I've learned and the strategies I've used to transform my life, my business, other people's lives, and their businesses for positive gain. Today, I'm happily remarried, have lost more than 70 pounds, race bicycles recreationally, have thriving business ventures, and take a completely different approach to life. Is my life perfect? Yes. Perfect in that I am lucky enough to have had the mentors, friends, and success strategies to transform my life. Now if you ask me if I am satisfied, I would say yes, but with the belief that life is about becoming a developing human spirit, learning, transforming, growing, contributing, and connecting in a wide variety of ways. I am, and will continue to be, a continual learner looking for ways to improve.

New question: "Am I perfect?" Answer: "Hell, no!" Not even close. I am just who I am. Are you overweight, in debt, or in unhappy relationships? Do you love your career, and are you happy with how you spend the majority of your time? Do you have beliefs that are holding you back, or are you too concerned about what other people may think if you make a change? Here's a tip for you: "If you have beliefs that aren't serving you . . . maybe it's time to get some new beliefs."

The statistics for obesity in America are staggering. Billions are spent in the weight loss industry on fad diets, weight loss pills, workout videos, and health club memberships, and yet the epidemic continues to grow. Let's put on our critical thinking caps for a moment. It's no secret how to lose weight. You simply have to burn more calories than you consume. If it's that easy, then why isn't everybody healthy, happy, and fit? Because we are a nation filled with the desire for instant gratification that is bombarded with the overabundance of processed food options that have been conditioned through poor habits, lack of discipline, and emotional eating patterns.

MAKE BETTER DECISIONS

Critical thinking is often characterized as an analytical way of thinking. It's using a more logical way to look at situations, evaluate the different options, and make conclusions. Critical thinking helps you make better informed decisions and is a skill set that you can learn and improve. Do you make most of your decisions emotionally or analytically? Looking back at my life, it's an easy answer for me: Emotions were a primary driver for years. Had I been more of a critical thinker earlier in my life, I would have saved more of the many millions I earned, built better relationships, not burned as many bridges, and been a lot happier a whole lot sooner.

Developing your critical thinking superpower is a key strategy for success. Taking the time to quickly analyze your different options, so you can *act* rather than react, will ensure you're making great choices that are moving you along in the direction you want to go.

Quality is never an accident; it is always the result of high intention, sincere effort, intelligent direction and skillful execution; it represents the wise choice of many alternatives, the cumulative experience of many masters of craftsmanship. Quality also marks the search for an ideal after necessity has been satisfied and mere usefulness achieved.
—*John Ruskin*

When you have to make a choice and don't make it, that is in itself a choice.
—*William James*

It's not hard to make decisions when you know what your values are.
—*Roy Disney*

Choices are the hinges of destiny.
—*Pythagoras*

Life is the sum of all your choices.
—*Albert Camus*

Using the power of decision gives you the capacity to get past any excuse to change any and every part of your life in an instant.
—*Anthony Robbins*

The doors we open and close each day decide the lives we live.
— *Flora Whittemore*

To decide is to walk facing forward with nary a crick in your neck from looking back at the crossroads.
— *Betsy Cañas Garmon*

Some Tips to Improve Your Critical Thinking Skills

1. Approach new problems with an open mind. Do your thinking on paper or leverage the superpower of mind mapping you learned earlier.

2. Define your desired outcome.

3. Get a clear understanding of the problem you're trying to solve. Aim to see the situation as it is, not making it better or worse than it really is.

4. Consider the situation from all angles and perspectives.

5. Do your research. Who else has struggled with a similar situation and solved it? What can you learn or model from those other situations?

6. Challenge your assumptions. Are they based on fact, emotions, or rational thought?

7. Define at least three options. If you feel you have no choice, then you create more stress, and your brain will not help you find a solution. If you think you have only two choices, then you'll have a dilemma. If you can expand your viewpoint and come up with three or more choices, then you will be empowered to make a better decision.

8. Make your decision and move forward.

PART 3

How Are You Going to Get There?

Congratulations! You know what you want. Now comes a big question: What do you do now? It's time to take stock and chart a path for the best destination of all: the person you were always meant to be.

Once you commit with certainty to making the journey toward your own destiny, toward your own best self, you will find that the steps get easier to take as you go along.

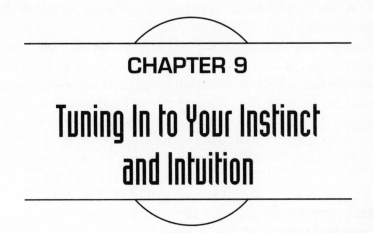

CHAPTER 9

Tuning In to Your Instinct and Intuition

Are you using your instinct and intuition to survive...or to thrive? For survival, we've been given the fight-or-flight instinct. It was necessary back in the caveman days if we wanted to stay alive and not get eaten by a lion or some other big scary creature. Now we don't have the same need in daily life to use this instinctual fight-or-flight response for personal survival, but to survive in business, it's still a dog-eat-dog world. One day you're doing great, and the next day you might be teetering on the brink of disaster. Do you choose between "fight or flee"? Or is there a third option? Could you possibly use your intuition and your instincts to thrive, to summon the very best from yourself, to achieve at levels that only a superhero could imagine?

As you know, I hold no medical or scientific degrees, or any college degrees, for that matter, but my life is living proof that there is indeed a higher power that you can tap into to guide your decisions and lead you to success. I've learned over the years to trust my instincts and intuition. My strategy has been to gather as much information as I can, within a reasonable time, and then let my brain incubate on the concept or situation. Every time that I was blessed with a strong intuition and followed it, everything worked out okay. The times when I went against my intuition usually didn't end up as well.

Developing your intuition is a true superpower. In 1980, I packed up everything I owned into a 1966 Chevelle and a 4-by-6 U-Haul trailer and headed south from Minneapolis. Two weeks before, I had decided to move to Colorado Springs, Colorado, to be close to the Olympic Training Center for speed skating. Another friend and speed skater, John DeBolt, was also moving there, and we planned the trip together. We drove straight through to Des Moines, Iowa, and then to Kansas City. We stopped for the night, and in the morning, John said, "Hey, I know a girl in Wichita that I like, and we don't have to be in Colorado for three more weeks. Let's go down and visit her; it'll be fun." We checked the map, and Wichita was only three hours south. Being adventurous and 19 years old, I said, "Sure, let's go."

Three weeks later, John decided he wanted to marry the girl and stay in Wichita. We were quickly running out of money, and I had to decide whether to continue to Colorado, go back to Minneapolis, or stay in Wichita. Now if I had opened up a U.S. map and picked a place to live, I don't think Wichita, Kansas, would've been on my top 10 list . . . or my top 50 list, for that matter. There was a top-ranked speed-skating team in Wichita, and after a few training workouts as a guest, I decided to stay for a while. And that little while turned into more than 30 years. Every time I was homesick for my friends in Minneapolis or was enticed to move to the east or west coasts, something strong inside of me compelled me to stay, and I credited it to my intuition. And usually within a day or a week of a big moving decision, I would get some amazing new opportunity.

Over the years, I've learned to quiet my mind and listen to my intuition. My instinct and intuition have served me well in many areas of my life. Do you listen to your intuition on a regular basis, or do you doubt your instincts? Often you hear people say, "I just have this gut feeling" or "I need to follow my heart." Regardless of what everyone else is telling them, they are firm in their beliefs and desire to move forward with whatever it is they are passionate about. How often do you listen to your heart or your gut to help you make wise decisions? How often has someone swayed you from following your instinct or intuition—and how has that worked out for you?

Are you utilizing your instinct and intuition superpowers? Or are you letting other people influence and change your decisions based on fear, not facts? I am not a fan of organized religion, but I certainly am very spiritual. I certainly do believe in a higher power. Consider that old saying: "Let go, let God." How often do you let go and listen to what your instinct and intuition are telling you? Les Brown used to say, "Leap, and grow your wings on the way down." Move forward in faith, and as you get new information, you always have the choice to change your mind or reevaluate to make a wiser, more educated decision.

Love nothing but that which comes to you woven in the pattern of your destiny. For what could more aptly fit your needs?
—*Marcus Aurelius*

It is a mistake to look too far ahead. Only one link of the chain of destiny can be handled at a time.
—*Winston Churchill*

If you don't know where you are going, you'll end up some place else.
—*Yogi Berra*

The only real valuable thing is intuition.
—*Albert Einstein*

Intuition comes very close to clairvoyance; it appears to be the extrasensory perception of reality.
—*Alexis Carrel*

Intuition is the supra-logic that cuts out all the routine processes of thought and leaps straight from the problem to the answer.
—*Robert Graves*

You have to leave the city of your comfort and go into the wilderness of your intuition. You can't get there by bus, only by hard work and risk and by not quite knowing what you are doing. What you'll discover will be wonderful. What you'll discover will be yourself.

—*Alan Alda*

I feel there are two people inside me—me and my intuition. If I go against her, she'll screw me every time, and if I follow her, we get along quite nicely.

—*Kim Basinger*

You must train your intuition. You must trust the small voice inside which tells you exactly what to say, what to decide.

—*Ingrid Bergman*

Trust your hunches. They're usually based on facts filed away just below the conscious level.

—*Joyce Brothers*

A hunch is creativity trying to tell you something.

—*Frank Capra*

The more and more each is impelled by that which is intuitive, or the relying upon the soul force within, the greater, the farther, the deeper, the broader, the more constructive may be the result.

—*Edgar Cayce*

Synchronicity is choreographed by a great, pervasive intelligence that lies at the heart of nature, and is manifest in each of us through intuitive knowledge.

—*Deepak Chopra*

I allow my intuition to lead my path.

—*Manuel Puig*

Intuition becomes increasingly valuable in the new information society precisely because there is so much data.

—*John Naisbitt*

It is always with excitement that I wake up in the morning wondering what my intuition will toss up to me, like gifts from the sea. I work with it and rely on it. It's my partner.

—*Jonas Salk*

Let's explore Tuning In to Your Inner Guidance

1. Be a continual learner. The fact that you're reading this book and exploring new ways to improve your performance and results validates that you're interested in learning.

2. Look back over your life, and consider how well you listened to your instincts and intuition.

3. Quiet your mind. Take moments each day to clear your mind of distractions. Find solitude where you can be in a quiet place without any interruptions. Turn off the computer, radio, and TV, and find solitude with yourself.

4. Practice being the observer. Stepping back from the situation will give you new perspectives and allow your intuition to assist you.

5. Follow your hunches. You will be amazed at the results you get.

6. Exercise your intuition. Your instincts are like muscles. The more you exercise them, the stronger they become and the more you can do with them.

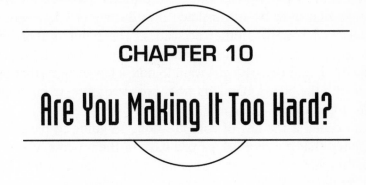

CHAPTER 10

Are You Making It Too Hard?

Do you sometimes wonder why other people achieve monumental success . . . and you're working just as hard, and are coming up with ideas that are just as good, but you're still struggling? Or have you ever seen some crazy product on an infomercial and said to yourself, "Hey, I thought of that!" Yet you're not the one collecting millions of dollars from the sale of that product. Those are clues that you need to look more closely at your process. Some of this may boil down to the difference between the can't-do and can-do attitudes. But some of the problem may also be in the strategies you are using to get where you want to go.

In my experience as the CEO of an integrated marketing company and business growth consultant, I constantly run across situations where people are making things way too hard and complicated for themselves. Now I suppose you could argue that it's easy from my perspective because I have vast experience in solving business problems like improving marketing and sales performance, leveraging the technology of the Internet, and improving bottom-line results. Maybe so, but as soon as the individuals learn to use tools and strategies I offer, they remark how easy it is now.

I mentioned earlier that I'm on the executive board of the National Speakers Association. This year, my friend Brian Tracy is also a board member. He is the chairman and CEO of Brian

Tracy International, a company specializing in the training and development of individuals and organizations. He's the author of 45 books that have been translated into dozens of languages, and he's received countless other accolades. The point is that he's a pretty smart guy. Although I certainly wouldn't reveal any specifics related to a board discussion, I want to note a few insights that Brian shared with the board members when we were going in circles on a specific topic area.

Brian called it the law of complication. 'm going to paraphrase, hHe stated that the more steps you have in the process, you aren't just adding more steps, you are complicating the process by a factor of five. Meaning, if you were to draw a graph and plot out the number of steps on the horizontal access, with the vertical access being the level of complication, each time you add a new step or element to the process, it increases the level of complexity by more than just one step. So if you have a process that has three steps, you have a complication value of 15. Add an extra step, and it doesn't just add an extra step, it increases the complexity another five points to 20. This is a simple illustration that helps us recognize we need to be aware of making things too complicated. If you want to make your life simpler, you can start by not making things more complicated.

Are you the type of person—or do you work for an organization—that seems to have too many levels of complexity, processes, or procedures? Let me be clear: I believe in creating processes and procedures to improve performance and produce consistent results. However, I also have to encourage you to evaluate your strategies, tactics, and performance results from time to time and ask yourself if there is an easier, simpler, or better way. Ask yourself, "Am I making this too difficult? Are there steps that I could eliminate or avoid and achieve the same or better results?"

I think it's interesting how many times in my life the answers to problems were right in front of me, yet because I felt that it certainly couldn't be that easy, it wasn't. I see this with the clients I work with on a regular basis. To help set the stage for a story, I need to give you a little bit of background. My target markets are organizations that want to find, attract, and keep their customers.

This includes corporations, entrepreneurs, business ventures, and associations. Corporations hire me to grow their business, and associations hire me to add value to their membership — commonly, business owners who are looking for strategies to increase sales and profits. Since I am a professional keynote speaker, author, and consultant on the topics of business success, Internet marketing, and innovation, I have attracted many other top keynote speakers and consultants as clients. They love to work with us because we understand their business model. We have vast experience in creating value propositions from intellectual how-to information.

One of my clients (I'll call her Sally) considers herself to be a sales and marketing expert, yet she has very little business. She joined my business accelerator consulting program to find help on growing her sales training business. That's not the uncommon part; I'm hired to help businesses grow all the time. What made this unique was that she wasn't implementing her own strategies from her training workshops and books. She wanted more business, yet she was making her lead generation efforts too complicated. During our first consultation call, she gave me all the reasons that her business wasn't successful anymore. She was convinced that ever since 9/11, organizations just weren't hiring outside speakers for their conferences, conventions, and events. She wanted more website traffic and sales leads, yet her website hadn't been updated in years. She wasn't active online on the popular social media websites; she didn't even have a LinkedIn profile. I asked her if she had a database of previous clients that she could use to prospect for new business, and she said yes, but it was outdated and in a variety of different places. She didn't have examples of her speaking in a demo video and didn't even have a YouTube channel.

I asked her about her referral network, and she said that she used to grow her business on referrals, but in recent years, the referrals had all dried up. As part of the business accelerator program, she sent me samples of her books and audio programs for review. Here's where it gets really interesting: The books and audio programs were filled with strategies and tactics to increase sales. On our next consultation call, I asked her, "When was the last time you read your own books or implemented those strategies?" After digging a little deeper, it was obvious that she was making things too complicated. She didn't feel very technical, resisted participating in any Internet marketing strategies, and felt that the strategies she had used for many years that helped her grow a thriving business wouldn't work anymore — strategies like cold calling, direct mail, article marketing, getting free publicity, and building her referral network. It's not that those tactics don't work in our information-overloaded, highly interactive, and technical world; it's that she needed to know how to integrate them into her daily activities in a fun and easy way. She was making her business too complicated. She was focusing more energy on why things would not work and the limiting beliefs that marketing in the new economy was too complicated, rather than believing in her expertise and how she could help others. As a sales expert, she needed to create her marketing and sales funnel and fill it with new prospects. With our help and guidance, she became able to transform her business, expand her reach, and generate new sales. We helped her find her inner superpowers, and she now has a thriving business again.

Reality TV can be a real time waster, and I would not recommend investing your time in it on a regular basis, but occasionally some true inspiration rises from it. I happened to catch a few episodes of the ABC show *Expedition Impossible.* It's a reality show from Mark Burnett, the creator of *Survivor.* It features 13 teams of three players each who travel across deserts, mountains, rivers, and exotic terrain.

One of the teams had a blind participant, Erik Weihenmayer. He was the first blind man in history to reach the summit of the world's highest peak, Mount Everest. During the episodes of *Expedition Impossible,* he had to ride horses and camels, scale mountains, jump off cliffs, paddle down rapids . . . and he could see absolutely nothing! How did he do it, and what the hell was he thinking? For that, you'll have to ask him, but he certainly was an inspiration. He exhibited these traits:

1. A can-do attitude and excitement for the thrill of the journey.
2. Complete trust in his companions to guide him.

3. Faith that if he followed through and just did it, everything was going to be okay. Was it a challenge for him? Probably. But as I watched him complete these tasks, he made it look easy. And his enthusiasm and excitement about everything made it look not only easy, but fun!

After watching him on the show, I Googled his name and found his web site, www.touchthetop.com. Check it out!

ENJOY THE RIDE

Do you live always with a can-do attitude? Are you filled with excitement? Are you enjoying the ride? Do you have complete trust in yourself, your team, your vision? Do you have faith to follow through and take the action needed to reach your goals and achieve success? Are you having *fun*?

Staples® office supplies stores had a moment of advertising brilliance when they branded around the concept "that was easy." I liked it so much that I even ordered Easy Buttons™ for our offices. If you feel like things are too hard, what would make the process easier? Put on your critical thinking cap, and make a list of things to explore. There are no wrong answers here, hopefully just a realization that life doesn't have to be difficult. You have the power to choose. Pick the hard way, or tap on your mental "I'm making this easy" button.

Are you the type of person who wants to make things too hard? Does your life seem like one long series of problems filled with struggles and heartache? Imagine what your life will be like when you adopt the superpower practices of this book, learn to let go, and unleash your inner brilliance.

> Life is not complex. We are complex. Life is simple, and the simple thing is the right thing.
>
> —*Oscar Wilde*

It is not because things are difficult that we do not dare, it is because we do not dare that things are difficult.

—*Roman Philosopher Seneca*

Any darn fool can make something complex; it takes a genius to make something simple.

—*Pete Seeger*

Man is not born to solve the problem of the universe, but to find out what he has to do; and to restrain himself within the limits of his comprehension.

—*Johann Wolfgang von Goethe*

A man must be able to cut a knot, for everything cannot be untied; he must know how to disengage what is essential from the detail in which it is enwrapped, for everything cannot be equally considered; in a word, he must be able to simplify his duties, his business and his life.

—*Henri Frederic Amiel*

Clutter and confusion are failures of design, not attributes of information.

—*Edward Tuft*

Don't make the process harder than it is.

—*Jack Welch*

Make Your Life Easier

1. List three things in your life that you feel are too complicated.
2. Write a few sentences describing your thoughts and observations related to each topic that you think is too complicated.
3. Ask yourself what steps could be eliminated that would allow you to reach the same result.
4. Practice making your life easier by cleaning out the clutter in your life, getting enough sleep, exercising, eating nourishing foods, taking care of yourself first, and not trying to please everybody else.

5. Be curious about life, and don't be scared to learn something new or to let go of something old.

6. Don't take yourself too seriously, have the capacity to laugh at yourself, and turn failure into fascination.

7. Focus on being productive, not just being busy. Don't mistake movement for productivity.

8. Learn to accept change as an integral part of life, as change is inevitable.

9. Don't wait for everything to be perfect. Work with what you have, where you are now in your life, and take massive action toward achieving your goals.

CHAPTER 11

Multitasking or Delusion?

You still hear a lot of people talking about how good they are at multitasking. Unfortunately, what they're really good at is deluding themselves. We are human beings, and human beings, whether they realize it or not, are built to do only one complicated thing at a time. That's just how we're wired. When we forget about that, all we really end up doing is distracting ourselves . . . and making ourselves less effective and productive than we could be.

This kind of distraction is a big problem today, and I think a lot of it connects to the way we choose to use our tools. Don't get me wrong. I am a huge fan of technology . . . when it's used properly. Sometimes, though, we use our technology in ways that just don't support us.

Are you really multitasking or just delusional about the amount of things you're accomplishing, and doing well?

LEARNED "ADD"

We are in a world right now where faster is associated with better. Many think that if you're not texting, typing, tweeting, reading, driving, eating, and watching TV all at the same time, you're not getting things done, or you might miss out on something important!

In reality, you're much less effective when you're not totally focused on the task at hand.

Look at us: We've got iPads, we've got iPhones, we've got laptops, and we've got GPS. We really have some amazing tools. All of this technology was supposed to make us more focused and more effective. In reality, what it's done for a lot of us is give us what I call learned ADD.

What is that? It's the kind of attention-deficit disorder that we train ourselves to take on. It gets worse and worse, and it actually makes us less and less effective, over time. But we think we're getting more done!

IS MULTITASKING WORTH DYING FOR?

One great example of what I'm talking about is the epidemic of texting while driving that we've got now. We taught ourselves to do that. When we have to put up billboards on the highways to remind us that we're not supposed to be writing notes to each other at the same time we're steering a two-ton piece of heavy equipment down a crowded interstate, then we know we've got a problem with learned ADD.

Delusion on the Road: A Matter of Life and Death

"I can check my messages while I'm driving. It only takes a few seconds."

Really?

Text-messaging creates a crash risk 23 times worse than driving while not distracted. (VTTI)

In 2011, 5,474 people were killed in crashes involving driver distraction, and an estimated 448,000 were injured. (NHTSA)

Sixteen percent of fatal crashes in 2009 involved reports of distracted driving. (NHTSA)

(continued)

(*continued*)

Twenty percent of injury crashes in 2009 involved reports of distracted driving. (NHTSA)

In the month of June 2011, more than 196 billion text messages were sent or received in the United States, up nearly 50 percent from June 2009. (CTIA)

Teen drivers are more likely than other age groups to be involved in a fatal crash where distraction is reported. In 2009, 16 percent of teen drivers involved in a fatal crash were reported to have been distracted. (NHTSA)

Forty percent of all American teens say they have been in a car when the driver used a cell phone in a way that put people in danger. (Pew)

Drivers who use hand-held devices are four times more likely to get into crashes serious enough to injure themselves. (Monash University)

Sending or receiving text takes a driver's eyes from the road for an average of 4.6 seconds, the equivalent (at 55 mph) of driving the length of an entire football field, blind. (VTTI)

Headset cell phone use is not substantially safer than hand-held use. (VTTI)

Using a cell phone while driving—whether it's hand-held or hands-free—delays a driver's reactions as much as having a blood alcohol concentration at the legal limit of 0.08 percent. (University of Utah)

Driving while using a cell phone reduces the amount of brain activity associated with driving by 37 percent. (Carnegie Mellon)

(*Source:* National Traffic and Highway Safety Administration.)

So lesson number one is pretty straightforward: Put the freaking phone down when you're driving. Your technology is not worth dying for...or killing someone for. I can tell you that, as a cyclist, I've been almost run over dozens of times by distracted drivers.

I don't know which is worse, drunk driving or driving while texting. All I know is that you shouldn't do either one.

ONE THING AT A TIME

I repeat: We can do only one complicated thing at a time—at least if we expect to do that thing well. And we are delusional when we try to stack tasks on top of one another and call what we're doing multitasking.

So that means we're actually wasting more time and attention than we should by leaving our e-mail open and jumping back and forth to check it every two minutes. We may think we're doing more work, but what we really need to do is block time out, turn off our e-mail, turn off our phone, focus on one thing at a time, and get the quality of our attention on that one thing just as close to 100 percent as possible for an extended period. Then, when it's time, we need to move on to something else, and we need to focus clearly on that.

STATUS ISSUES

Now, I know that a lot of people are going to be tempted to push back against what I'm saying here because they're in love with this idea of themselves as being more efficient when they zip back and forth at a hundred miles an hour. They've built that myth of multitasking right into their self-image, into their professional identity. For a lot of people, it's a status issue. The more screens they have open at the same time, the more things they imagine they're doing simultaneously with their technology, the more important they feel, and the more valuable they think they are to their organization.

That's a myth. Take a look around, and you'll notice that the people who are most valuable to any organization are the people who have trained themselves to focus on one thing at a time. If you really want to enhance your status in the organization, you want to do what they're doing: one thing at a time.

And you know what? The people who make phones and tablets and laptop computers and so on haven't really challenged that myth that multitasking equals status. Why? Because the myth helps them sell more of their equipment.

I'm all for selling cool tools, tools that do what they're supposed to do, but sometimes I think we need to make more distinctions about what really works and what isn't currently working in our lives. That's really one of the main points of this book, so I really hope you're not going to be one of those people who choose to buy into the multitasking myth, who choose to make themselves less efficient and productive.

And by the way, if you run into someone who does buy into that myth, someone who reads this part of the book and says, "What are you, Ford, a PhD in psychology?" then you can tell that person my answer: No. I'm not. But this guy is.

There is no such thing as multitasking—at least not the way you may think of it.... Multitasking, as most people understand it, is a myth that has been promulgated by the "technological-industrial complex" to make overly scheduled and stressed-out people feel productive and efficient.... Multitasking involves engaging in two tasks simultaneously. But here's the catch. It's only possible if two conditions are met: 1) at least one of the tasks is so well learned as to be automatic, meaning no focus or thought is necessary to engage in the task (e.g., walking or eating) and 2) they involve different types of brain processing.... [For instance,] your ability to retain information while reading and listening to music with lyrics declines significantly because both tasks activate the language center of the brain.... You simply can't talk on the phone, read e-mail, send an instant message, and watch YouTube videos all at the same time. In fact, when you think you're cruising along the information highway, you're actually stepping on the gas then hitting the brakes, over and over. (Jim Taylor, PhD, "Technology: Myth of Multitasking," *The Power of Prime*, March 30, 2011)

ZIPPING IN AND OUT OF PARKING SPACES

Some people can think really, really fast, jump from one topic to another, and then repeat the process. And some other people have strengths that go in other directions. Shouldn't we play to our own strengths? Absolutely. But at the same time, we don't want to kid ourselves about how much we're getting done or how we're spending our personal resources. As Jim Taylor suggests, we have to get a little clearer about how much gas we're really burning, how often we're slamming on the brakes, and where we're actually going.

Yes, if we want to, we can choose to zip in and out of 30 different parking spaces in the same parking lot for half an hour. That's our right. We can do that. But we need to ask ourselves: Are we getting as far in that half hour as we would if we pulled out of one parking space and then spent 30 minutes driving, with full, focused attention, to the next destination on our list? Then, when we pulled into the next parking space, we would have gotten somewhere. We would have accomplished something with that half hour!

DON'T DING!

I once had someone in my office who would leave his phone on all day long. And every single time he got an e-mail, his phone dinged.

No matter what he was working on, as soon as that phone dinged, he'd pick it up and look at it. Well, the distraction and the lack of focus were costing him literally hours of productivity every day. But he had deluded himself into believing he was being more efficient by doing what he was doing! After auditing his time on projects, I saw he was more than 50 percent slower on tasks than the other team members. I tried to coach him to improve and turn his phone off, yet he just didn't want to do it. In the end, I gave him an opportunity for new career development elsewhere. Yes, I fired him.

Now I tell people in my office: Turn your e-mail off . . . and you'll get more done! My motto is "one thing at a time . . . to 100 percent!"

So that's one big, specific, incredibly important takeaway that I want to leave with you: Schedule specific times to check your e-mail during the day, and don't break that schedule. You'll find that life won't end if you're not constantly interrupted by your e-mail.

Follow this one simple idea, and you'll improve your productivity. Set your phone on vibrate, and tell people to call you, rather than e-mail you or text you, when they have a true emergency. Then focus on one thing at a time.

MANAGING INTERRUPTIONS

If you are constantly interrupted, how do you expect to get anything done? Interruptions come from more than just texting, calls, and e-mails. What about your work environment? Are you constantly interrupted by your coworkers? Now, as we discuss interruptions, I want to clarify that I'm not talking about customer inquiries or important communications. I'm referring more to managing your interruptions. Everyone in my office knows that a sales inquiry deserves immediate attention and is not an interruption. When our phones ring, we have a receptionist and specific call groups to route the calls. When the phone rings, we call it "the Money line." However, when it comes to e-mail, we have specific times blocked for reviewing and responding.

I've always prided myself at Prime Concepts for having an open door policy. For years, I encouraged my employees to come to me whenever they had a question or concern. The problem was that in the beginning, I didn't set any boundaries or guidelines. Now, each one of them has a spiral notebook titled "Ford list." Here's how it works. During the day, they capture items they need to discuss with me in the notebook, and then I have specific block times when we meet to cover their questions. We use the ABC method: *A* means that it's absolutely necessary, *B* means that they need an answer or resolution before a specific date, and *C* means it can wait. This helps them prioritize their needs and has definitely improved the performance and productivity of our team.

As an innovative thinker programmed on how to make things better, I sometimes get off track on tangents and go to training mode. For example, Katie came to me to review a 65-page document of website content for one of our clients and just needed my review and approval. As I reviewed the content, other ideas came to me about how she could learn more about keyword research and integrating specific keyword phrases to help Web pages rank higher in the search engines. Katie recognized that I was going to get off track, and since she's been trained in how to manage interruptions, we moved that training task to the parking lot. The parking lot is a place to capture ideas and thoughts that we don't want to forget but don't necessarily need to be taken care of at that moment. I have a large whiteboard in my office for a parking lot, and we have the walls in our main conference room and in our think tank conference room painted with dry-erase whiteboard paint to park agenda items. (The brand of paint we used is from www.ideapaint.com. It turns virtually anything you can paint into a dry-erase surface that becomes a hub of creativity and collaboration.) Using the ABC method time, the parking lot has given us many more productive hours each week.

STAYING FOCUSED IS A SUPERPOWER

Speaking personally now, I can tell you that since I first noticed the learned ADD pattern, I've gone in the direction of using only one tool at a time, with one window open at a time, to work toward attaining one goal at a time. And I can tell you without any doubt at all that I am getting much more done, faster, and producing much better results.

A weakness of all human beings is trying to do too many things at once.

—*Henry Ford*

Multi-tasking arises out of distraction itself.

—*Marilyn Vos Savant*

Multi-tasking: Screwing everything up simultaneously.

—Anonymous

The simple act of paying positive attention to people has a great deal to do with productivity.

—Thomas J. Peter

In an industrial society which confuses work and productivity, the necessity of producing has always been an enemy of the desire to create.

—Raoul Vaneigem

Ask yourself: How much of the time and energy available to me am I wasting each day by jumping between tasks?

Ask yourself: How many years have I been conditioning myself, after years of using computers, to have multiple windows open at the same time and to jump between windows?

Ask yourself: How well is that way of working serving me? Does it play to my strengths? What would happen if I tried working in a different way for one straight day and compared the results?

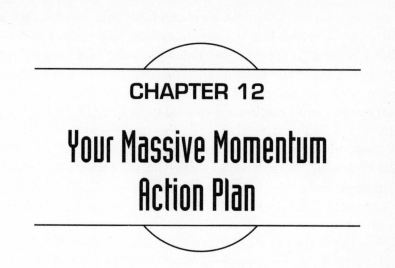

CHAPTER 12

Your Massive Momentum Action Plan

By this point in the book, I hope you've learned a little bit about creativity and innovation, as well as done some self-discovery. You've learned a couple of tactics concerning what you need to do differently to make your life better. That's not enough, though. You need to have an action plan.

This is your massive momentum master action plan, or MMAP. You can't expect to get anywhere on this journey without a MMAP!

A good MMAP is built around the principles of leverage and clarity. When I work with people to get them to do a marketing plan, a business plan, or any type of strategic plan, I make sure I get leverage before I do anything else. I want to find out what it is they want in life, why they want it, and what they are going to do. You have to be absolutely clear about why you're doing what you're doing. You have to have leverage! This concept of leverage is so important that I've devoted the entire next secion of this book to it...but you need to understand a little bit about this principle in order to create any kind of workable plan. So we're going to focus on leverage now, too.

By now, you've got your success mind-set, your superpowers are engaged, you're thinking prosperously, you have a clear vision of what you want to achieve, you know the value you have to offer, you have a multitude of ideas and solutions to help you add value to earn your success, you can put your critical thinking cap to work, your instinct and intuition are kicking in, you've tapped the "easy" button, and you're focused. *But...* you may not have leverage yet. So what you need now is a massive momentum action plan. Your MMAP is what you will use to move yourself forward and make it all happen!

Your MMAP consists of clearly laid out steps to achieve your clear vision for success.

How big is your goal? Do you want to lose 10 pounds, become a best-selling author, transform your business from a shop to a corporate dynasty? Or perhaps you're the CEO of a Fortune 500 company and want to see sales increase over the next five years by at least 20 percent a year.

You have a goal, you have a target market (or multiple markets) you want to reach, and now let's get a plan in place to make it happen.

My favorite way to get started on a massive momentum action plan is to use mind mapping. This can give you a one-page snapshot of all the moving parts and pieces that will be involved to execute your plan.

> "A mind map is a graphical way to represent ideas, concepts and strategies. It is a visual thinking tool that helps structuring information, helping you to better analyze, comprehend, synthesize, recall and generate new ideas.... Since it is an activity that is both analytical and artistic, it engages your brain in a much, much richer way, helping in all its cognitive functions." — Luciano Passuello, "What Is Mind Mapping?" (www.litemind.com/what-is-mind-mapping)

Whether you decide to use a mind map or follow some other format, you have to come up with the initial plan—a brain dump of everything you think you want to do. No one else can do that for you.

The next step is to categorize those different ideas into no more than five or six sections and then prioritize the outcomes you want. You should become very outcome focused, not task focused. Now I have to ask: What do you have to do? What does success look like? What do you have to do to get that outcome? What are you willing to do that's lifestyle friendly? That term *lifestyle friendly* means, for example, that I can tell you how to lose weight, but if following those steps are not lifestyle friendly to you, you're not going to do it.

So it's all about selecting the activities that are congruent with what you're willing to do and your goals. Your motivation comes from the level of pain you have that you want to make go away or from the specific desire or pleasure you want to achieve. Everything that we've done in my business, when it comes to launching a new product line, includes writing a massive action marketing plan for it. We determine the outcomes, specific strategies, milestones, and timelines. Every website project we developed, every Internet marketing campaign or social media campaign, starts with deciding our desired outcomes. We plan around those outcomes, and we define and use predetermined metrics to measure it. That's the same basic theory that this entire book is about: The book is the plan and the different pieces are the sections.

You can create a MMAP for virtually any goal or outcome you want in your personal or professional life. For example, a client came to us who was going to be speaking to a new group in a few weeks, but she didn't have any specific products they could purchase after her presentation to help them continue their journey of learning. She knew, though, that she could help them continue to make improvements even after her presentation. Together, we used the MMAP process to help her build and visualize the plan for the new product she could offer to that audience.

I called the meeting planner (I'll call her Deb) and asked her to give me details about the group and the presenters they had hired in the past. Deb described a group of pharmacy owners and pharmacists who typically spend only a couple of hundred dollars when they attend her events. She mentioned that they were very conservative, so if we were going to offer them a information product resource, like an audio program, it couldn't cost over $197. I asked her for a few names of the pharmacists who would be attending the Florida event. She e-mailed me a few links to their websites and their contact information. I thanked Deb for her feedback and insights, but in my many years of marketing, I learned that it's never really a price issue; it's a value issue. People spend the money if they see the value.

So I interviewed a few people who were planning to attend the conference and discovered that they were definitely interested in ways to transform the culture of their workplaces and grow their businesses. Now this particular speaker client of mine did specialize in business transformations, so I went through the massive momentum action planning process to outline the new video training product and the strategy to sell it. She didn't have the video content yet, but she said that she could definitely present on the topic area.

She had only a couple of weeks before she had to give her presentation; there was virtually no time to develop the content, video and edit it, or design the packaging of the physical product. Here's what we did: My team designed a small tabletop display and ordered it from postupstand.com. We designed attractive colored promotional flyers with a mock picture of the product, title, and sales copy and two-part order forms that we would distribute during her presentation. Other than the cost of designing the flyers, display stands, and order forms, which was an investment of under $500, we were set.

I called the client back and said, "I've got your product concept and outline done, it's going to be sold for $997." She was confused and said, "You mean $97?" and I said "No, $997." She replied, "That won't work, it's too expensive, and the meeting planner said they typically only spend a couple of hundred bucks. If we offer it for $997, no one will buy it." But I insisted, "We've got a good plan. Let's work with it, and let the market tell us what works."

She said, "Okay, great, I've got the content, but we don't have a product." I said, "Don't worry about the product. If you take the signs and order forms to the event, and you don't sell anything, don't worry about it. We won't produce it. But if you take it and sell it, then we will produce the new product, and it will be well worth the effort."

The plan is set. The date of the presentation comes, and she flies to Florida to present to the pharmacy group. Three-quarters of the way through her presentation, she mentions, "If you like what you've heard here and you want to continue the journey, come see me. I have a special resource that can help you implement many of the concepts we've covered today when you get back to your organization."

I got a call from her when she was at the airport to fly home, and she just said, "Oh, I love you, I love you, I love you. We just sold 95 packages at $997." That was over $90,000 of product sales from an audience of only 400 people the meeting planner thought would never invest that kind of money on resources. This experience isn't an exception. I've found that many times so-called experts give poor advice not backed up by experience or real numbers, and those lack or limiting beliefs put restrictions on what's possible.

Now, she still had to produce the product, but with $90,000 in orders, she could certainly afford to spend a couple of days in the studio shooting the footage. All she had to do was go into her office with a video camera and film 12 30-minute video segments. She sent us the raw video footage on a USB drive, and my team at Prime Concepts Group edited it, added the intro/outro, designed the product packaging, created the virtual digital download versions, and produced the finished product. You can check out the product called "Breakthrough Business" at her website, RoxanneEmmerich.com. Keep in mind that she had all of the valuable content and booked the speaking engagement; what we did was leverage her intellectual property and create a new value proposition...because of the MMAP.

If it's a more individual problem, if you're someone who hasn't started a company yet but wants to get your career on track, your mapping process would start with doing a prosperity dream board and getting really clear on what you want to do, have, or become. You have to make a really clear picture in your mind of what you want first and then put it on paper. You can't do the plan without the outcome.

Here is a great resource for you to create a prosperity dream board. It's from one of my partners, Randy Gage, and it comes with everything you need. Here are the details.

RANDY GAGE'S PROSPERITY MANIFESTATION MAP KIT

This is the prosperity manifestation map or dream board that you may recall Randy discussing in his prosperity books and his *Prosperity* audio album. A prosperity map is a big poster (22 by 28) that you fill with images of things you want to do, have, and become.

Seeing the images you placed on it every day programs them into your subconscious mind. This creates a desire within you to take the daily action steps that bring your dreams closer to reality. You see your prosperity in your mind first, and then you manifest it on the physical plane.

Start collecting magazines, brochures, images from the Internet, and other materials in the hobbies and areas you are interested in. Randy suggests you divide your map into sections such as work, spiritual, relationships, wealth, fun, and fitness.

There are no rules for how you put things on the prosperity map, except that the image has to mean something to you. It doesn't matter if anyone else understands it. They don't need to, as long as you know what it means every time you see it. Get ready to have a lot of fun with this very powerful tool for manifesting your prosperity.

No excuses: This Prosperity Manifestation Map Kit comes with scissors, marker pen, glue stick, and complete instructions from Randy on how to get the best results, so you can start immediately. The whole kit is regularly $20, but as a reader of *Superpower!*, you can get your Prosperity Manifestation dream board kit for only $10. Why so cheap? Because I'm the publisher of Randy's products, and I want you to have this superpower tool. Claim yours now at www.SuperPowerBook.com. Okay. Back to the MMAP process.

Once you have the outcomes captured, you need to put the strategies and tactics of the plan in writing. Think on paper, not in your head. If there's a point here to the general public or to a 22-year-old who's just starting a company, it's to think on paper. Create your capture list, categorize the items into sections and subsections, and estimate what resources you'll need and the timelines. This sounds elementary, but you'd be surprised how many people complain about their poor results, yet they don't have a written plan of attack or take action to improve their situation.

Create your written plan, but make sure you have a set of measurements in place to check and see if you're on track, so you can make the necessary course corrections. Then the key is to be able to work the plan and use your feedback and metrics to determine whether the plan is working.

For example, when I was a speed skater at the Olympic Training Center, we had very specific nutrition, fitness, and strength training coaching program plans. Those plans helped me and the other athletes compete at top levels in the nation. Then I went into competitive cycling and started a family. When I'm operating my life within a plan, things go well. But when I got too distracted, had conflicting goals, or lost my focus, things gradually fell apart. You've no doubt heard of the term *self-sabotage,* right? That's what happens when we lose focus or our beliefs aren't in alignment with our actions. I'm far away from being perfect and have my share of baggage and flaws, too. However, by using the strategies and tactics I'm sharing in this book, I've been able to overcome many obstacles, attract the love of my life, and add tremendous value to my clients, which is rewarding on many levels.

I'm 50 years old now, and I recently joined a triathlon club to help me get back in better shape, not because I want to be super competitive in triathlons, but because I want the structure and disciplined action plan. As soon as I joined the club, they did an analysis of where each of us was with our fitness level and asked us why we wanted to do it to get leverage. Then they gave us a nutrition plan, a flexibility plan, and a strength training plan. That's a MMAP right there.

The key is to set up a plan that excites you enough to make you want to take action on it every day, no matter what. Consistent daily action is the key. If you're trying to use water to make a dent in a rock, it's better to put an eyedropper full of water on a stone every day for a year than it is to dump a bucket of water on it once. Small consistent efforts are generally better than rare moments of brilliance.

On the topic of visualization, even if you don't consider yourself a visual learner or you have a different learning style, it does help to have actual visual stimuli attached to your goal. I'm a firm believer that even people who say they aren't visual are, actually, pretty visual. It's possible that you're not going to agree with everything in this book, but don't tell me it doesn't work until you've tried it.

It's just like everyone else that I work with in business. I go in to work with some of the top CEOs in the country, and I come up with ideas that are totally against what they're used to doing, what schools teach them, or anything they've heard in the past. I say to them, "Don't tell me this idea or concept isn't going to work unless you've tested and tried this before." The point is to challenge the assumption to see if it's grounded in fact or opinion.

I want to encourage you to not skip this step. You might be thinking, "Oh, I know all this," but where is your dream board? Where is your prosperity board? Do you have it on your computer? Do you have the pictures of what you want to do, have, or become? Is it on a screen saver? Do you have it on your phone? Is it printed out? Do you really have a truly clear idea of what you want in the different roles of your life?

Use these tools to get clear about your unique answer to the question: How do you want to live your life?

Remember, this isn't about acquiring stuff; it's about becoming. You might achieve serenity, become a great parent, or give back to your community or a philanthropic cause—anything. My point is that I truly believe that the purpose of life is to be a developing human spirit, and to do that you need to be continually learning.

That's what I want this book to help you with, to give you insights on how to unleash your inner superpowers to improve the quality of your life and the lives of those around you.

If you're missing some formal credential that people usually expect to see, don't worry about it. I believe that a big part of my success was that I only had a formal ninth-grade education. I was on a special work-for-grades program in high school. This was an alternative for troubled kids who were most likely going to drop out. During senior high school, I was required to go to school for one hour a day in the morning and then go get a job where the employer would complete a quarterly attendance and performance report card. Being the innovative kid that I was, I figured out that if I started my own business, then I would be my own boss and be the person completing the report cards and submitting them to the school. The education I received in starting and running my own business at age 15 certainly gave me a quick education filled with unique challenges that other 15-year-olds weren't solving, like where to get clients, how to market services, how to track sales, accounting, inventory control, job costing, and finding employees. Yes, finding employees.

When I had Saeks Painting and Light Construction, I had three crews working for me, and my employees' average age was 45. When I hired new people, they thought a parent must own the business. When I told them I was on my own, they were shocked initially, but they didn't care as long as they had steady work. I kept them busy and split the profits with them. They taught me about the processes and painting, and I kept them working with a full schedule.

When I started doing things in my business, I did them because I wanted to. I didn't know you weren't supposed to do things a certain way. I had no idea of what the rules or proper strategies were. I didn't have any self-imposed limitations, even though many adults at the time said that I was too young to run a business. I thought, "Too young for what? I'm making the sales calls, arranging the proposals, bidding the jobs, invoicing, and collecting the money."

When I first joined the National Speakers Association (NSA), an association dedicated to the working professional speaker, I followed everything they told me to do for the first year . . . and I lost money. It wasn't because what they taught was wrong; it just wasn't right for my specific situation.

Then I went back and said to myself, "Wait a minute! I know how to brand, market, how to sell, I know how to add value," and then my business took off like a rocket. I'm now proud to be on the national board of NSA and was just reelected to a second term. Over the years, NSA has provided enormous learning opportunities and a community in the form of networking with other professional speakers. If you've ever thought of becoming a professional speaker, or you are one now and want to take your business to the next level, then you should check out the local chapter meetings or attend one of the popular national conventions. Learn more at www.nsaspeaker.org. If you want to learn how to get paid to speak, then you must visit www.GetPaidtoSpeak.com. It's a membership website dedicated to helping individuals learn how to get paid for their expertise and intellectual content. It's run by Darren LaCroix, a world champion of public speaking, and me, Ford Saeks, a business growth strategist, author, and acclaimed professional speaker. Okay, back to the point. Don't let excuses or another person's limited vision become your reality. Create the plan, work it, modify it as necessary, and get on with it already.

There should be something you can see that brings your success into existence before you start executing the plan. I apply it toward everything in my life. For example, before I wrote this book, I made a mock-up cover design of it and hung it in my office. Before I even submitted the book proposal to the publisher, I designed a book cover and media release. Before I was successful in business, I wrote headlines about myself and visualized them appearing in my favorite business magazine; before I went to the Olympic Training Center, I told myself that I was going to compete at an Olympic level. And I did!

A few years ago, I was hired to present to Global Spectrum, a subsidiary of Comcast. Global Spectrum manages public assembly venues and arenas in the United States, Canada, the Middle East, and Southeast Asia with an ever-increasing international presence.

The company hosts a wide array of popular sports and entertainment events, trade shows, performing arts, and other special events. I was first hired to present to Global Spectrum's area general managers and sales and marketing teams. Their offices are in Philadelphia, and I found out they worked closely with the Philadelphia Flyers of the National Hockey League (NHL), the 76ers National Basketball Association (NBA) team, and some farm league teams for hockey and baseball. When I returned home from the presentation to the marketing personnel, I thought how cool it would be to actually provide marketing insights for an NBA and NHL team.

Soon after thinking about them and adding their logos to my prosperity manifestation map, I received a call from Global Spectrum and the teams' marketing managers to prepare and present customized training for the Flyers and 76ers group ticket sales teams. I was flown to Philly a couple of times and got to attend a Flyers hockey game and a 76ers basketball game as a VIP. Do I think that adding their logos to my dream board was some hocus-pocus? No, but I do believe that I attracted that opportunity into my life through focused effort and my MMAP. Not to get too magical, but I do believe that we attract things, people, and situations into our lives that we focus on. If you're mainly tuned in to a negative channel of thought, I can guarantee that you'll manifest pain and negativity into your life. Through visualization and an action plan, you can transform your life.

This pattern has played out for everything significant that I've ever accomplished in my life. When I projected it, my mind went there first, and then my body and the world worked to manifest it.

You can do a very simple sketch. It doesn't have to be fancy or cost a lot of money. You just have to have a clear vision of why you want something and make sure it's congruent with all of the other things and specifically your actions in your life—because you can't have two conflicting goals and expect to get to your destination. You also can't just think about things; you have to get off your butt and take massive action. The key is to have a plan so you aim your efforts in the right direction.

Taking the time to create your massive momentum action plan is one of the most important and critical steps to your success. With your plan in place, you will be superpowerful, confident, and ready to move forward toward your goals. In fact, *action* is a superpower. Being able to take action and execute the steps in your plan is what will make the difference between a life of quiet desperation and one of health, wealth, and fulfillment.

Are you ready to create, visualize, and take action on your plan? Good. Get started!

Create a definite plan for carrying out your desire and begin at once, whether you are ready or not, to put this plan into action.

—*Napoleon Hill*

Bite off more than you can chew, then chew it. Plan more than you can do, then do it.

—*Anonymous*

A goal without a plan is just a wish.

—*Antoine de Saint-Exupery*

Make no little plans; they have no magic to stir men's blood.... Make big plans, aim high in hope and work.

—*Daniel H. Burnham*

A good plan, violently executed now, is better than a perfect plan next week.

—*George S. Patton*

Plans are only good intentions unless they immediately degenerate into hard work.

—*Peter Drucker*

It is a bad plan that admits of no modification.

—*Publilius Syrus*

He who every morning plans the transaction of the day and follows out that plan, carries a thread that will guide him through the maze of the most busy life. But where no plan is laid, where the disposal of time is surrendered merely to the chance of incidence, chaos will soon reign.

— *Victor Hugo*

Have you gotten your prosperity map dream board kit? (YES/NO)

Have you made your brain dump capture list? (YES/NO)

Have you sorted and categorized items based on your roles, goals, and dreams? (YES/NO)

Have you created your massive momentum action plan? (YES/NO)

PART 4

Getting Leverage

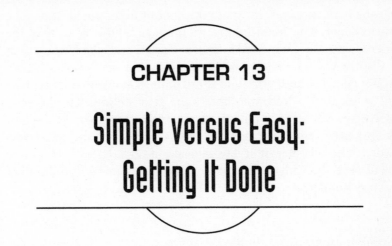

CHAPTER 13

Simple versus Easy: Getting It Done

From this point forward, I am assuming that you know exactly what you want to accomplish most in your life. (If you don't, it's time to take a break and revisit some of the earlier sections of the book.) Now what you need are some tools that will help you get additional leverage and start making measurable progress toward your goals. You need some strategies for moving forward and gaining momentum.

That's what this next part of the book is all about. If you have made it this far, you are ready to be personally accountable for taking action on your own plan. You are not part of the vast majority of the herd who sit on the sidelines and make comments about what other people do out there in the game of life. You are ready to take the field and run a play. And I am here to tell you that once you become one of those people—the people who regularly take action on their behalf, the people who get leverage on themselves—you have joined a pretty exclusive club. You have become someone who takes responsibility for your own outcomes. So if that's what you're here for . . . congratulations, and welcome to the club.

It is not the critic who counts; not the man who points out how the strong man stumbles, or where the doer of deeds could have done them better. The credit belongs to the man who is actually in the arena, whose face is marred by dust and sweat and blood, who strives valiantly; who errs and comes short again and again; because there is not effort without error and shortcomings; but who does actually strive to do the deed; who knows the great enthusiasm, the great devotion, who spends himself in a worthy cause, who at the best knows in the end the triumph of high achievement and who at the worst, if he fails, at least he fails while daring greatly. So that his place shall never be with those cold and timid souls who know neither victory nor defeat.

— *Theodore Roosevelt*

Something many be *simple,* yet *not easy.*

Surprise, surprise: It's actually simple to do the things we know we need to do to move forward toward achieving our goals. For example, the strategy for losing weight is simple. Cut down on the calories you consume, exercise more so you burn the calories, or do both. The process is (structurally) simple . . . *but it's not necessarily easy.*

The same thing goes for the business sector. The strategy to make money in business is simple. Really, when you get right down to it, there are only four possible ways to make more money with your business. They are:

1. Get more customers.
2. Increase the frequency of purchases.
3. Increase the average transaction value.
4. Lower your operating expenses.

And that's it. That's all there is to it. End of business class, right? Well, maybe not. Like the weight loss example, the strategy that works may be simple enough, but executing it is not easy in practice. This is where it becomes important to identify what you're not great at and then find resources that can leverage your time. It's an incredibly important self-management tactic. You have to find the way to get the best results with less effort.

How do we get that done? There are three steps:

1. Understand your core competencies.
2. Buckle down and actually do the work.
3. Delegate the work to someone.

And when it comes to delegation, that process is done most effectively after you've deleted all the distractions and figured out what *you* have to do; then you can really know what to delegate and outsource. Ask yourself: "What better use could I make of my time?" I have someone who cleans our house, someone who cleans our pool, and someone who mows our lawn. Why? Because I delegated those responsibilities.

That's a big step in leveraging your success and making progress on the stuff that looks simple, but isn't actually easy: using delegation strategies.

PLAYING TO YOUR STRENGTHS

For you, getting leverage might mean finding a partner or outsourcing: finding someone who can do what their core competency is better than you can and giving them some kind of compensation for it. Even though we have a team of competent professionals on staff, we utilize virtual assistants and outsource certain tasks. With the advances in technology, especially videoconferencing, Skype video calls, GoToMeeting sessions, base camp HQ project management, and cloud computing, it's easier than ever to utilize talent around the globe.

Knowing what your core competencies are is absolutely essential. It means knowing exactly what your fastball is, so to speak. You need to know where your strength lies and spend most of your time and energy, your wattage, and your power on that. In business, I believe people are good at one of these three areas: *marketing* (selling something), *management* (operations), or *making something* (producing a product or providing a service). At best, you may be competent in two of the three, but rarely are you strong in all three areas. For example, I understand management and operations, but my strengths are in marketing and delivering innovative marketing and sales campaigns. If you're in business or in business leadership, you need to have a broad spectrum of knowledge, including your brands, products, services, industry, value propositions, and competitive advantages, but to be effective, you need to leverage your strengths.

While writing this book, I was reminded of this life lesson again. We had an accounting controller who had worked for me for several years. Each year, I delegated a few more responsibilities, with less oversight and accountability. The lesson I'm referring to is that delegation is certainly a superpower, but you must delegate with oversight and accountability. This person decided that even though we had employment agreements, noncompetes, and confidentiality terms of employment in place, he could embezzle funds, work on his extracurricular activities at work, and attempt to create tortious interference (mess with our clients). So while I'm a fan of delegation to other staff members, JV partners, or virtual assistants, please make sure that everybody involved knows what success looks like and that the results are measurable.

I'm not a big believer in strengthening your weaknesses. You should learn from and grow out of your weaknesses, but you do need to focus the majority of your time on your strengths. Getting into the habit of playing to your own strengths is another one of those things that sounds simple . . . but actually isn't easy. You have to build up the muscle. You have to do it over and over again until it feels like second nature.

At the end of the day, I believe the first and most important step when it comes to getting leverage on yourself is not to make the mistake of thinking that because something is simple — because you understand it — taking action is easy. Until you've practiced using your superpowers, taking action on your goals may not be easy. It takes work, it takes persistence, and it takes deciding to get back up after someone or something knocks you down. You just have to make the decision to settle in and do the work you love, delegate the work you don't, and then take steps that support you. What's the alternative? Really, there's only one: setting up and reinforcing a habit of avoidance. You know the kind of habit I'm talking about: We set aside time on our calendar specifically to make some kind of forward progress on our goal, we're just about to take action . . . and suddenly we decide that it's really, really important to start vacuuming the rug. Or cleaning out the refrigerator. Or checking our e-mail, Facebook, and LinkedIn pages.

This is what's called *approach avoidance,* and it means, essentially, doing everything *but* what you're know in your heart that you're supposed to do. You have to delete the distractions and either do something or delegate something. That's what I mean by getting leverage. Don't let distractions be an excuse for not getting done what you need to get done.

TAKE CONTROL OF YOUR DAY

To plan your day and prioritize your tasks, you have to know how to say no to nonessential tasks and break down larger tasks into smaller categories and more manageable tasks. Just the effort of putting ideas into categories in chunk sizes reduces your stress and keeps you more productive. It's a method of evaluating how you're spending your time.

Keeping a journal — in your case, your Superpower Guidebook — is one of the first and most important steps of good time management. This one tool will help you lose weight, close sales, or do anything else you need to do. When I work with salespeople, I have them time themselves with a stopwatch while they're on the phone selling or face-to-face with a client. At the end of the day, I have them add up how much time they *actually* spent selling, and most of the time it ends up being less than an hour a day. Most of the rest of their time is taken up by extraneous activities that they thought contributed to selling but, in actuality, weren't as important as communicating to prospects and clients. The same analogy works with marketing—you have to limit your distractions and block out your time effectively. That means getting plenty of sleep, dieting, and exercising. You have to make sure that you're healthy, and there are plenty of resources available to help you do that.

Many people talk themselves into believing that they are productive when they're actually not. They're just busy. We have to steer away from that delusion. A lot of times, the best way to meet this challenge is to find a partner to keep you on task and accountable by discussing your actual allocations of time during the day. (See the later discussion on mentors, where I look at this subject in more depth.)

You're on track, and it's time to execute. Now the question is how the work that needs to happen gets done. Do you have the skills and talent to do it all yourself? Who on your team can you delegate tasks to so your projects and goals can move forward? Have you established a realistic time line for accountability?

Time management is a superpower. Don't just be busy. Be productive. Take action on your goal. Run and play.

Take time to deliberate; but when the time for action arrives, stop thinking and go in.

—Andrew Jackson

An ounce of action is worth a ton of theory.

—Anonymous

Well done is better than well said.

—Benjamin Franklin

The shortest answer is doing.

—Lord Herbert

Trust only movement. Life happens at the level of events, not of words. Trust movement.

—Alfred Adler

We should be taught not to wait for inspiration to start a thing. Action always generates inspiration. Inspiration seldom generates action.

—Frank Tibolt

When I stand before God at the end of my life, I would hope that I would not have a single bit of talent left, and could say, 'I used everything you gave me.'

—Erma Bombeck

Over the past week, how many times did you . . .

. . . say "no" to nonessential tasks? _____

. . . break down larger tasks into smaller categories and more manageable to-do items? _____

CHAPTER 14

Cloning Time: Leveraging Technology

Y ou and I are extremely lucky, because we are living in a period of human history like no other. What makes this period of time so different? Like I've mentioned before, our technology. It is connecting us to new ideas, new communities, new solutions, and new tools at mind-bending speed—and it's giving us access to resources that seemed unthinkable just a few years ago.

So here's the deal: We have a choice. We can leverage our new technology and harness its power in support of our goals. Or we can ignore that technology and keep doing things the way we've always done them because that's what we're familiar with.

I say we should embrace the change, harness the technology, and put it to work because the other option, the option where we stick with what's familiar, just costs too damned much in terms of our time. I hope you feel the same way, because once we make that decision, we will find that almost *anything* that we decide we want to achieve can get done easier, faster, and with less stress . . . *if.*

If we choose the right tools. If we use those tools for the right purpose. If we stay focused. If we invest just a little of our time in keeping up with the latest technological solutions, the solutions that really support our goals.

Those are some big *if*s. And those *if*s are why I wrote this part of the book. This section is all about mastering what may be the most essential twenty-first-century skill of all: choosing and implementing the technology that supports your goals and gives you more time to pursue them.

NEW TECHNOLOGY ISN'T SCARY

Now, I realize that even the phrase *new technology* seems scary to some people. But the *reality* of new technology isn't scary in and of itself. If it were, I don't think we would be texting each other and sending each other messages on Facebook as often as we do.

If you plan to put the principles of this book into practice, you must learn to move past any limiting labels and beliefs you may have about technology, and you must make a personal, ongoing commitment to use new technology to win back more hours in your day. Fortunately, mastering the *right* new technology isn't scary at all—or at least, it is only as scary as you want it to be. Once you decide you don't want the experience to be scary, you are ready to . . .

LEVERAGE TECHNOLOGY TO CLONE YOUR TIME

"Wait a minute. What did he just say? Can technology really *clone time*?"

My answer is yes, absolutely!

How is that possible? How can you use technology, specifically information technology, to clone your time? Well, you're literally holding the answer in your hands. The book that you're reading right now would not exist without the time-cloning power of today's technology.

When I was writing this book, I found myself under some serious time pressure. I knew exactly what I wanted to say in all the chapters, but I just didn't seem to have all the weeks in the calendar that I needed to turn it into the finished manuscript that I was supposed to deliver. And there was another factor I had to deal with: My publisher, John Wiley & Sons, was pretty serious about the deadline because they already were promoting it and taking preorders on Amazon. Bottom line: Three weeks away from my drop-dead date, I had the chapters outlined, but I had only about half of my manuscript written in print-ready format.

With my busy keynote speaking calendar, running Prime Concepts Group, multiple projects and consulting clients, countless joint venture (JV) deals, cycling, and, let's not forget, having a happy home life, I found that I had underestimated the time necessary to write a 60,000-word manuscript. No, I'm not complaining, because everything is a choice. The point was that I needed to utilize more of the strategies I teach on a regular basis. I had slipped into old habits, and I just didn't have enough time to keep on doing what I was already doing. So what did I do? I started doing things differently. I started looking for ways to clone the time I had. There were lots of options. In this particular case, I cloned my time by talking into a telephone that was connected to a special website I found.

I used an electronic dictation service called Cogi.com. There are a lot of good dictation services out there, and any number of them could have helped me to reach my goal, but Cogi.com was the one I chose, based on the recommendation of a friend. Cogi.com lets you call into a telephone number, talk your brains out, and then request verbatim transcription of what you just said on the call. That transcription is done by a real human being, and it comes back to you in text that you can easily paste into a Microsoft Word file. With the help and support of a friend, I decided to start using Cogi.com.

Four hour-long talk sessions and three calendar days later, I had 60,000 words of text to work with, which my assistant then pasted into four Microsoft Word files. Now, mind you, those were very rough files. They were not in any way, shape, or form ready for me to turn in to my publisher. But those transcripts of me talking about exactly what I wanted to see in the unfinished chapters of the book were what my assistant and I needed to get started. They dramatically sped up the process. Once we had those files, we were ready to edit and refine the text. To make a long story short, I hit my deadline.

Now, notice the steps I went through:

STEP ONE: I identified exactly what it was that I wanted to accomplish: Complete my manuscript by a certain date.

STEP TWO: I identified the kind of tool that could help me clone my time and attain the goal: A dictation service.

STEP THREE: I got a recommendation from a trusted source about a specific piece of technology that matched that description and would actually work. This part is important, because if you don't have a recommendation from a trusted source that a certain tool not only works but also is easy to use, you may end up wasting a lot of your time. That's the opposite of cloning time, of course. If you find your tools are wasting your time, you need to change tools, quick!

STEP FOUR: I got to work, and I didn't get distracted until I got the outcome I needed.

I followed all four steps carefully, and guess what happened? That three-week deadline that looked so impossible suddenly became possible. I got as much done in three weeks as I would normally have been able to get done in six. I finished the book . . . because I cloned my available time.

YOU CAN DO IT, TOO

You really can clone your time, just like I did. You just have to follow the same steps.

Now, what typically happens the first time people try this process is that they lose momentum when they get to step three. They stop in their tracks, because they don't know what tool to pick. There are a thousand tools out there to choose from, and you may not have good recommendations yet about what's likely to work for you as you pursue your goal.

I have two solutions for this problem, and both of them are easy to implement. Here's the first solution: read the following section, where you'll find my own list of great time-cloning tools that I can personally vouch for from personal experience. (I'll share the second solution with you when we get to "Finding Time-Cloning Communities," a little later on.)

THREE GREAT TIME-CLONING TOOLS YOU CAN USE RIGHT NOW

Note: The fact that something appears on the list doesn't mean it is the only, the best, or the most efficient tool for cloning your own time and achieving your own goal, but it does mean that I have used it successfully to clone my time and achieve my goals and used it with my clients and that I can vouch for it from personal experience.

Your SmartPhone

If you don't have a smartphone, which is an Internet-enabled cell phone like the iPhone or Android, you need to get one. If you already have one, you can probably find new time-cloning uses for it. (But remember, not while you're driving!) The smartphone I can vouch for personally is the iPhone, and I recommend it highly, thanks to its ease of use and the vast number of apps available for download. People now tend to use their smartphones primarily for four things: texting, e-mail, surfing the World Wide Web, and connecting with others on social media platforms like Facebook. Way behind the field, in last place, is actually making telephone calls. There is a whole lot more you could be using your smartphone for in terms of cloning your own time and pursuing your goals: Cogi.com, for instance, has an iPhone app. (See also the later discussion of the iPad and its apps because many iPad apps run on the iPhone.)

Some Kind of CRM System

One of the tools that has really helped me clone my own time (and the time of others who ask me for advice) is a customer relationship management system (CRM system). This is a powerful database program that you use every day to keep track of people, schedules, sales funnels, and events. Think of it as an electronic Rolodex that puts all the information you need about managing relationships with your prospects, customers, and schedules right at your fingertips, instantly. If you're not using such a system, you need to start, and you'll see how powerful it can be for your business. We use a popular program from Sage, called ACT! It keeps everything up-to-date and in sync on my iPhone and iPad by means of CompanionLink software (http://www.companionlink.com/ipad/act/). A couple of other great CRM options are SalesForce.com and Infusionsoft.com. There are literally hundreds of options for CRM, and the point is to get one if you don't have one and to learn how to really leverage it if you already have a CRM solution.

An iPad

Why am I suggesting that you get yourself an iPad, rather than telling you to buy some other name-brand tablet computer? Because I love my iPad, that's why, and because I would have to think hard if I were given the choice of never using an iPad again and never using my right arm again. I am not the only one who feels this way about the iPad. When this revolutionary product first came out, tech writer Rory Marinich had one of the most widely circulated quotes about it, a quote I still love: "Apple's not actually selling a computer. Or a flash drive or multitouch. They needed to make those things for their product, but that's not what the product is. The product is, simply put, a magical screen that can do anything you ever want it to, no matter what that is." A few years on, the magic has only gotten more breathtaking. Apple's detractors may like to make fun of quotes like Marinich's, but the reality is that this tool has transformed our daily lives, and several industries, for one simple reason: People find it easy to use and love using it. That is definitely something to consider when you are looking for tools that can clone your time: Do you love using it? If you do love using a certain tool, and if you choose the right tool for the job, there is a pretty good chance that the tool will help you become more productive. That definitely beats using technology that you hate, which is what most people who don't have iPads do. Does it replace a laptop or desktop computer? Maybe not. Does it clone your time? Yes.

MY TOP "SUPERPOWER" IPAD APPS

Back in the old, pre-iPad days, you may remember, a personal computer ran software that came on disks. You popped the disks into your computer, and you copied the stuff laboriously. It could take about an hour, maybe even more if you ran into a system problem. In other words, you *began* the process by burning time. The software was expensive, and it usually boiled down to three or four broad, deeply boring functional areas: word processing, spreadsheets, database management, and presentations.

On the iPad, there are literally thousands of specialized applications (apps), most of which are very cheap (as in well under $10) or even free, and all of which you can download with lightning speed. Right now, I am willing to bet you a steak dinner that one or more of those thousands of apps is specialized to match up with something important that you want to make happen in your life. That means your magic screen is, in all likelihood, just a 10-dollar bill away from lining up perfectly with some goal for which you need to win some more time. So what are you waiting for? Visit your smartphone's app store, and see what's out there. Or you can use my list of my own favorite apps.

When it comes to iPad apps, and even iPhone apps for that matter, you can't always judge the price as an indicator for quality. There are several free apps that outperform apps that charge. Many apps offer trial versions or standard and pro versions. When selecting your apps, take a few moments and look at the reviews and ratings to get an idea of other people's experiences before you download them. A popular tactic that companies are using is to allow you to download and use the app and then select an upgrade to buy new features while you're inside the application. With the popularity of the Android phones and other digital pads hitting the marketplace, you'll have to do your own due diligence and find out what works best for you and your devices. You don't need to download and use each and every app. Remember, don't get seduced by the dark side of technology. Be a critical thinker. Review the list, and download the apps that you feel would best suit your particular needs and lifestyle. The apps I've listed focus more on productivity and performance than on social interaction or lifestyle. For me, the more productive I am, the more free time I have to enjoy a better quality of life. Here is a list of my top 13 iPad apps, not in any particular order.

1. **Notability:** I love this app because it allows me to capture audio and notes at the same time. I use it for simple tasks: taking notes because it allows me to also draw on the screen using my finger or stylus or just type text. I use it when I attend seminars or during client consultations, and it allows me to easily color-code my documents. I've used several of the top productivity apps as of this writing, and Notability performs the best. Learn more about Notability at www.Gingerlabs.com. I use another popular app, called Evernote, to hold notes, ideas, photo snapshots, and recordings, complete with geolocation tagging of pictures or notes. Evernote synchronizes with my Mac and Windows desktop computers, too. A couple of others that you may want to look at are Notes Plus and Penultimate, but Notability and Evernote are my favorites.

2. **GoToMyPc:** I love this app and also the desktop versions for remote access of my computer systems. I simply haven't found an easier way to be productive and keep all of my files in one place. Like many busy executives, I utilize a laptop, an iPad, and my network computer system. Now when I travel, I carry just my iPad because I know I can use GoToMyPC

to access desktop files. I also use GoToMeetings from my iPad for group conferences with my employees or during consultations when I want to present information to the group using one shared computer screen. GoToMeetings has added video conferencing while screen sharing, and that has improved the performance and effectiveness of our communications (www.gotomypc.com).

3. **GoDocs for Google Docs™:** Many of you know and love Google Docs and use it all the time. GoDocs for Google Docs on your iPad, iPhone, or iPod Touch allows you to easily interact with your Google Docs library in a meaningful way. It extends Google Docs functionality to your iPad; this app allows you to store and then subsequently edit and share all of your documents, regardless of format. More advanced features like the ability to add multiple Google Docs accounts means being able to segregate your work documents from those that are personal while accessing them from the same devices. I love the layout and functionality of this app, and it certainly qualifies as a superpower app. If you're new to Google Docs, go to docs.google.com to get started. Then download the GoDocs for Google Docs app, and you'll be up and running in a flash.

4. **Documents to Go™ Premium Office Suite:** If you use Microsoft Office, this is the "must have" collection of utilities for accessing your Office files on an iOS (smartphone or digital pad) device. You can create, edit, and view Word, Excel, and PowerPoint files and sync to Google Docs, Dropbox, Box.net, iDisk, and SugarSync. And you can view PDFs and sync files between a desktop PC and your iOS device (www.Dataviz.com). An honorable mention is necessary for **QuickOffice Pro HD** (www.QuickOffice.com). It's very similar to Documents to Go and has some very nice features, too.

5. **Pages Word Processing:** This app, part of the iWork Suite, allows me to create, edit, and view word processing documents on my iPad and iPhone. It syncs with my iCloud

account and helps keep my documents up-to-date across all of my devices. I'm mainly a Windows user, although we have several Macs in our offices. Using Pages allows me to easily work between Microsoft® Word and Apple's Pages files (www.apple.com/apps/pages).

6. **Keynote:** The best way to describe this app is to compare it to Microsoft PowerPoint. It's the Mac's best tool for creating, editing, and viewing visual slide presentations. Now with the newer versions of the iPad and iPhone, you can use full-screen mirroring to present directly onto an HDTV or with an LCD projector. I use Keynote on my iPad in small face-to-face meetings. Using Apple video output adapters, I've even been able to present innovative supporting visuals during my business training presentations. Certainly worth a mention is Apple's Numbers App. If you have to create, edit, or view spreadsheet files or work with Microsoft Excel files on your iPad, then you'll want to get the Numbers app, too (www.apple.com/apps/keynote and www.apple.com/apps/numbers).

7. **Skype Video Calling:** For many years, we utilized Skype and our offices to support our international clients, and lately, we've been utilizing Skype as a primary method of communication within our offices, with our clients, and even during sales calls. This allows us to make free video calls or calls to other phones and not tie up our incoming switchboard phone lines. The power of face-to-face communications helps improve our performance and results. Being able to use my iPad, I can easily connect with other Skype users and make face-to-face video calls. Apple has a similar program on the iPad and iPhone called Facetime, but I prefer Skype because it works on a wide variety of systems and not just Apple devices. When we work with new clients and they've never used Skype before, we'll send them a web camera if they don't have one, and use GoToMyPC to configure it. We use it for instant messaging, too. This improves our relationships with clients in our local

market who would come into our offices and meet face-to-face (www.Skype.com).

8. **PrintCentral Pro:** Using PrintCentral, I can print direct to most Wi-Fi printers or to all printers and any document type via my Mac or PC. I can view, store, and print e-mail, attachments, documents, files, photos, contacts, and web pages and even copy items from other apps that I want to print. You can transfer docs and files via iTunes using USB cable (Apps Tab), open documents stored in PrintCentral directly into iWork (Mac's productivity suite) for easy editing, open files stored in the cloud (iDisk or WebDAV service) directly into iWork, and open and print files directly into PrintCentral from any other app that supports the "Open in . . . " file-sharing features. I've tried several other "print from iPad" devices, and this one is definitely the best one I've used so far. They have several other cool apps, too. You can learn more about them at www.EuroSmartz.com

9. **Dropbox:** I and many of my staff members and clients consider Dropbox to completely change the way we store files, especially when working between different computers and networks. Dropbox for iPad takes advantage of the screen and also gives you previews of your documents, photos, and media. You can open your documents in whatever app you have installed that supports that type of media. I use it to keep file versions that I'm working on updated. For example, while working on this book project, I used Dropbox for the manuscript. That allowed me to open the file and edit it on my iPad, my office desktop, and my laptop. This app is an extension of the services provided at www.dropbox.com, where you would set up an account and then select who gets access to what folders. Keep in mind that if you plan to use Dropbox extensively, you'll be adding files to "each" device locally, and then Dropbox syncs it across all platforms. For example, we were working with a client to produce their product promotional videos. They added the clips to their Dropbox account and then gave Prime Concepts

access to that specific Dropbox folder. That immediately added many large video files to all Prime Concepts computers that utilized that particular client's Dropbox. It posed no real problem; we just copied them out of Dropbox to our network, and that removed them from the other computers that didn't need to share the files. This sounds more complicated than it is, and you'll find this a great superpower tool for sharing files and keeping then in sync.

10. **MindManager** Mind Mapping: we've already discussed the power of mind mapping in an earlier chapter. A quick reminder, though, is that mind maps are a great way to capture ideas, recall them faster, and communicate them to others more effectively. The computer program, iPad, and iPhone that I use for mind mapping is from www.Mindjet.com. In the iTunes store, you will find many mind mapping software apps. For instance, another popular mind mapping app is iThoughtsHD by CMS (www.ithoughts.co.uk). iThoughtsHD will import and export mind maps to and from many of the most popular desktop mind map applications. For those of you who crave an app for creating outlines, check out OmniOutliner. Whereas iThoughtsHD and MindManager are more free-flowing, OmniOutliner is a structured thought organizer, excellent for taking notes or organizing thoughts into subsections and bulleted outlines (www.omnigroup.com/products/omnioutliner).

11. **Pocket Informant:** Pocket Informant HD is a fully integrated calendar and task solution for your iPad that lets you focus on everything you do in a day–not just your tasks list. You have the power to change virtually every feature to suit your specific preferences. The calendar feature that comes standard on the iPad is really poorly designed. It doesn't allow the flexibility necessary to manage calendar features across different devices. Yes, it's free and works for simple tasks related to calendar functions, but the services and features provided by Pocket

Informant take it to the level that I would have expected from Apple (www.PocketInformant.com).

12. **iBooks and Kindle Book readers**: iBooks is Apple's book reader, and the Kindle app allows me to read the books I purchased through the Amazon Kindle store on my iPad and iPhone. I use my iPad so much that I literally gave away my Kindle. I may be a bit old school and enjoy having the physical book, too, but having access to my book library on my iPad is great. I'm a big believer in buying the physical version of an important book, though, because it's a more tangible interaction, and when I put the book on the book shelf, I am reminded of it whenever I see it. I can pass the physical book to a friend or colleague or take notes in the margins. Are you going to buy every book in physical form? Not anymore. It's no secret that bookstores are closing all across the nation and that newspapers are practically extinct. I have more than 100 books on my iPad's Kindle app. That means that, on long plane flights, I have everything I want to read at my fingertips without having to carry heavy books. Best of all, when someone mentions a book, I can jump onto the online store, and a couple of clicks later, the book is in my hand. Both the iBooks app and Kindle reader app allow bookmarking and highlighting. You can get the Kindle app in the iTunes store, and you can learn more about it at www.Amazon.com. The iBook app comes standard with the newer iPads, and you purchase books through iTunes at www.iTunes.com. Personally, I prefer the Kindle app because the Amazon book selection is unbeatable.

13. **Social Media Apps for personal and business use.** All of the popular social media websites, including YouTube, Facebook, LinkedIn, and Twitter, have mobile apps. Social media can be a huge time waster if you're not careful, but it's quickly becoming a normal part of modern societies. Human beings want to connect, and social media has transformed how we interact online and even off, too. It has changed buyer behaviors and the way that businesses listen, connect, engage, and service

their customers. If you're a business owner, you'd better have best practices in place and have your company and brand established and monitored using social media. The last thing you want is an unhappy customer to utilize the enormous power of social media to hurt your brand or image. I use social media apps on my iPad to filter conversations and alert me to new opportunities. For example, I use HootSuite for Twitter to schedule tweets and sort keyword phrases and hashtag (#) phrases I want to monitor. Recently, a friend of mine had a problem with Comcast for his cable service, and he tweeted #Comcast, #fail, and a short complaint. Within minutes, he was direct-messaged by Comcast customer service asking how they could help solve his issue. That was after he sat on hold and was transferred around, ending up in voice mail hell. One tweet and minutes later, he was getting his situation resolved. Now that's superpower! One note of caution: Before you post anything online anywhere, remember that every device has a unique IP address and can be traced back to you or your accounts! Okay, moving on: I love the YouTube app because it gives me direct access to the billions of videos on YouTube. Google owns YouTube, and they want to send traffic to YouTube, so if there are relevant videos on YouTube, they will come on the first page of Google in the search engine results page.

Leveraging technology is an extremely important skill. But you should only be using technology if you know what you want to get out of it. I tell every one of my staff members to not ask their supervisors about how to do things with software like Microsoft Word or Excel because the answer can be found online with maybe 10 minutes' worth of research. Don't waste anyone's time with that stuff! Years ago, you had to call tech support or ask someone, but today, leveraging technology means using the resources already at your fingertips. The only reason some people can't get used to doing it is that they'd rather use YouTube for different purposes that don't have anything to do with the goal or with what we're trying to do. For people to work together effectively, they need to know what they can do now and what steps they need to take to expand their knowledge base.

There are all kinds of resources on YouTube, LinkedIn, Facebook, and elsewhere — communities you can tap into to find answers. So leveraging technology means leveraging all the available resources in the activities you're going to be involved in, whether it's for a business goal or a personal goal.

Okay, by now I'm sure you get the point. Get connected, get an iPad, take the time to explore the apps, and then start downloading and experimenting with your superpower critical thinking cap on.

THE TWO BIG REASONS PEOPLE GIVE FOR NOT CLONING THEIR TIME

From where I sit, there are two big excuses that people give themselves for not getting the most out of technology that could win them more hours in the day to achieve their goals. Excuse number one is "I'm not a computer person" or the variations "I'm not an Internet person," "I'm not a social media person," "I'm not a tech person," or whatever. And excuse number two is "I'm so busy, I don't have time to learn about any new technologies." Let's look at each of these.

First, "I'm not a technology person." If you stop to think about what you actually did with your time over the past, say, 72 hours, you can probably debunk this one yourself. If you watched TV, if you've ever played a video game, if you've ever posted anything on Facebook, if you've ever sent a text message, or if you've ever watched a video on YouTube, then you already know that *some* of the technology that's available to you is incredibly easy to use. That's a big part of the reason you watched a show, played that game, made that post on Facebook, sent that text, and watched that video: It was so easy. Right?

So I think what people really mean when they say something like "I'm not a technology person" is "I only like new technology that is as easy and intuitive and fun as the technology that I am already using and enjoying." Well, guess what? There are all kinds of technology out there that are just as much fun and just as easy to use as what you are already using. You just need some help finding it and getting started.

The second big excuse I hear is "I don't have time." In fact, people get pretty emotional about this one. They don't just *say* they don't have time to connect with new technology: They insist on it!

My question for all the people who offer me this reason: Do you have time for learning about or using any other technology during the day... technology that *doesn't* support you in achieving your goal?

For instance, the average American watches an average of four hours of television each day. Do you have enough time to watch funny videos for 30, 60, or 90 minutes of your day but not enough time to watch a video about how to quit smoking?

Do you have enough time to take part in an online community that's devoted to making fun of the mistakes celebrities make in their personal lives but not enough time to join an online dating service so you can find the perfect mate?

Do you have enough time to complain online about something that happened to you at a job you hate but not enough time to join LinkedIn and make the professional connections that will help you get a new job and take your career to the next level?

Almost every time I push just a little bit on this excuse, what I find is that the person I'm talking to has plenty of hours available, hours that are being allocated to technology that has little or nothing to do with the person's goals. In other words, people allow themselves to get conditionally distracted. Here's the good news: You can fix this problem pretty easily, just by joining a new community and using technology a little more strategically than you're using it now.

FINDING TIME-CLONING COMMUNITIES

A little earlier, I shared some of my own favorite time-cloning tools, and then I promised you a second solution for the situation you face when you don't have good, specific time-cloning recommendations. Here it is: Find a virtual community that has people who know how to pick — and use — the right technology. Become part of that community. Make some alliances. Get some recommendations. *Don't get sold a bill of goods*: Get multiple recommendations from multiple people with credibility, and see how those recommendations stack up.

Two of the more obvious communities you should consider joining are the professional networking service LinkedIn (www .linkedin.com) and the freelance portal eLance (www.elance.com), which is a great place to find practical experts on any number of fronts. Of course, there are a thousand other online communities you can join that can help you clone your time, but those two are particularly rich sources of allies, best practices, and connections. The communities you want to spend your time in are the ones that align with your goals.

The really beautiful thing about finding the right time-cloning community is that sometimes you find that you don't have to master any new technology at all in order to get the outcome you want. Let me share a personal story that will give you an example of what I mean.

A while back, I paid almost $20,000 to get an iPhone app made. The programmer got halfway done with the project...and then became a missing person. I was frustrated because I had invested all this money and had nothing to show for it. So now I had a problem. I figured I would join a community, pose a question, and get some sense of how best to fix it.

I went on to elance.com. I posted a question: "Hey, I'm looking for someone to finish this iPhone app. It's almost done. Here's the app. Give me a bid on whatever you think you can fix it for."

A guy wrote back and said, "I think I can do if for $75 — maybe $150, tops."

I hired him for a $150. He did more for that incredibly low fee than the other guy did for 20 grand! And he finished it up in a hurry. That gives you some sense of the awesome power of the online community.

You could make the argument in the other direction, of course, and point out that I should have gone to eLance first to get a more competitive bid. And you would be absolutely right. There are any number of ways to get ripped off in this world; I believe joining the right virtual community, and then posing the right questions, is now mandatory if you want to avoid being one of the people who gets ripped off. I've heard horror stories from elance.com, too. You can avoid them by doing your due diligence, checking references, and not paying until the project is complete. Case in point: social media consulting. Lately, one of the most popular ways to get fleeced is to hire a so-called social media expert who will share, for a stiff fee, all kinds of inspired wisdom on this subject that you could, and should, very easily find on your own. Everybody and his brother are now claiming to be social media consultants, but most of these firms will be out of business within a year or so of the date they pitch you because they don't understand business, relationship building, or how to influence and connect with an online community.

Yes, of course, you can leverage your time and hire a social media marketing services firm to set up, syndicate, and integrate your digital footprint online, but no one will understand your business and customer needs more than you. You or someone qualified and competent on your team needs to guide your value propositions, set your goals, and monitor progress. It's important that your branding and voice on social media are congruent with your organization. Social media offers many benefits for you to listen to the marketplace, identify new opportunities, and connect with, engage, and influence your target prospects.

A FINAL THOUGHT: USING TECHNOLOGY STRATEGICALLY

Virtually any problem you can think of, any question you have, or any challenge you face can be resolved by leveraging the technology at your disposal. I'm talking about the truly strategic use of the technology you now have at your fingertips. Someone else has probably solved the problem before you and has left the solution for you as a present.

I know a teacher who no longer writes lesson plans: He downloads and updates dozens of great lesson plans that show up, free for the taking, on teacher websites. I know salespeople who no longer battle with receptionists: They use their existing contact networks to gain direct, person-to-person access to CEOs via LinkedIn. I know executives who have solved major business problems by modeling what another company in another industry was doing. This is leveraging technology. Anything—and I mean anything—that you have to solve to attain your goal has some kind of solution online. Your job—your privilege—is to use today's technology to track down that solution and see whether it makes sense for you and whether it supports you as you move toward attaining your goal.

Let me give you just one example of the vast, untapped power of the technology that is at your disposal right now. To understand how big a deal this particular use of technology was, you have to understand that I was single until I was 35 years old. I grew up as an orphan in the housing projects of North Minneapolis. For most of my life, I didn't cook. Period. If it didn't say unwrap, place in microwave, and rotate every 30 seconds, I didn't bother with it. Yes, I know, it was a terrible strategy.

One evening about six months ago, I was at home all alone. My wife called. (She's the one who normally cooks, and the food is amazing. The deal is that she cooks and I clean up.) My wife says, "Hey, I'm running late, and I'm not going to make it home in time to make dinner."

I said, "Okay, honey, what do you want me to do?"

She said, "Well, there's chicken, there's defrosted chicken in the refrigerator. I need you to bake the chicken, put the potatoes on, and make dinner. Can you handle that?"

I said, "Sure."

Now, I'm 50 years old, and believe it or not, I've never baked a chicken in my life. I didn't want to embarrass myself, though. So the first thing I did was pick up the phone and try to call my best friend, Steve. Steve knows how to bake a chicken, and he's a great cook!

I get voice mail. No Steve. Now I'm screwed. She's going to be home in an hour, and I don't know how to cook. I thought about going to get takeout, but didn't want to take that option.

I grabbed my iPad, went to YouTube.com, and typed in the magic words: "How to bake a chicken." In five seconds, I received the search results for several videos on how to bake a chicken. I selected a video that showed me exactly how to bake a chicken, step by step. Put it in a pan, preheat the oven to 350, put specific spices on the chicken, add some oil, put in the washed potatoes, and cover it with tin foil. I kid you not, I prepared the whole dinner from watching YouTube clips. It was ready when she came home. She took one look at the table with the full meal I had set and walked straight over to the trash can. She started digging through the trash.

I said, "Honey, what are you looking for?"

She said, "The takeout bags." She actually thought I had ordered from a restaurant, thrown away the containers, and then put it on our plates! Oh, ye of little faith! The problem now is that she expects me to cook more often, which actually has been a dream. We are spending more quality time together, and the food tastes so much better.

What do I mean by leveraging technology? Leveraging technology simply means using YouTube, Google, Facebook, Twitter, and all the other great resources out there to learn exactly what you need to learn to achieve your goal—fast. If leveraging technology can help me achieve something seemingly impossible—like baking a chicken before my wife walks in the door—imagine what it can do for you!

> The first rule of any technology used in a business is that automation applied to an efficient operation will magnify the efficiency. The second is that automation applied to an inefficient operation will magnify the inefficiency.
>
> —*Bill Gates*

> Congress should pass a law restricting public comment on the Internet to individuals who have spent a minimum of one hour actually accomplishing a specific task while on line.
>
> —*Andy Grove*

These technologies can make life easier, can let us touch people we might not otherwise. You may have a child with a birth defect and be able to get in touch with other parents and support groups, get medical information, the latest experimental drugs. These things can profoundly influence life.

—Steve Jobs

If you are facing a challenge or obstacle in your life, find out what resources for solving it can be found on the Internet. The power of what you can find on websites like YouTube for video instruction is amazing. More than 20 hours of content are being uploaded to YouTube every minute! The next time you have a question, type it into the YouTube search box, and I bet you'll get amazing results.

CHAPTER 15

Mentorship Magic

Superman and Jor-El. Spiderman and Uncle Ben. Luke Skywalker and Obi-Wan Kenobi. Just about every great superhero has a mentor... and you should be no exception. Mentors are the key to unlocking our superpowers. Once you have the right mentor, you have a special kind of role model: someone whose example helps you when you need guidance most, someone who makes it easier for you to learn and grow from your weaknesses, someone who can help you maximize your strengths and get the help you need in the areas where you lack expertise.

Having a mentor *rocks*.

Most people don't realize it, but there are really three different kinds of mentors. Once you learn to take full advantage of all three kinds of mentor relationships, you will have access to new levels of power, influence, self-confidence, and authority that most other people only dream about. You become a different kind of person: the strongest possible version of you. It's almost like magic. In fact, from a distance, the quantum leap you will take in your life will look so much like magic that that transformation might as well *be* magic.

The magic of mentorship emerges from three very different sources:

1. A coach who challenges you helps you set goals and holds you accountable for getting the most from your own talents and capacities.
2. A mastermind group.
3. Someone who is not personally known to you, but who serves as an important role model, and whose life, career, and decisions you study closely. (This person may be alive or dead.)

Let's look closely at each of these three groups now.

MENTOR GROUP ONE: COACHES

When it comes to getting a professional coach, the purpose for you is twofold. You've got personal, one-on-one accountability, as well as identifying a leader for you. In my professional life, I've hired coaches for accountability training, business growth, and leadership expertise.

This kind of mentor can offer advice and help you learn to hold yourself personally accountable for making the changes you need to make. The most popular example of this kind of mentor is the entrepreneur or executive who takes a promising young newcomer on as a protégé. Andrew Carnegie, for instance, was mentor to Charles M. Schwab, the first president of U.S. Steel. One of my favorite books is *The Compound Effect* by the publisher of *Success Magazine,* written by Darren Hardy. He credits many of his success strategies to his mentors, like Jim Rohn and others.

You can also work with a whole different kind of coach, someone who has a skill or capacity that you don't. Here, the mentor is not so much helping you grow as filling a gap for you. Although there is still the potential for you to learn from the relationship, both you and the mentor expect the mentor to take action on your behalf—and do stuff you aren't in a position to do.

Whether you choose a professional coach or an expert with a certain area of expertise, you want someone who's going to tell you the truth, someone who's not judgmental, someone who's a critical thinker and willing to call it tight. You want someone who will challenge your assumptions and help you spot your own BS. I have had several great individual mentors—the legendary author, educator, and consultant Nido Qubein being one. Each mentor is in my life for a different reason, fulfilling a different role, but all have helped me unleash and develop my potential. It's an ongoing journey.

A common mistake people make with coaches is to assume that it is the coach's responsibility to ensure that you achieve your goal. It's not. It's yours.

> My success was due to good luck, hard work, and support and advice from friends and mentors. But most importantly, it depended on me to keep trying after I had failed.
>
> —*Mark Warner*

MENTOR GROUP TWO: MASTERMIND GROUPS

For my business, I prefer to work with groups of accountability masters who help to hold *each other* accountable. There is a common variation on this kind of mentor relationship, commonly known as a mastermind group. A mastermind group allows participants to both lead and follow, to act as both mentor and mentee, depending on their skill set and the situation they face.

I've been a member of many mastermind groups over the years, and I've created my own inner circle mastermind groups. In these programs people invest up to $10,000 and must meet certain conditions to be a member. Want to know why? Because people will pay large sums of money to get great ideas and solutions to their problems and then be held accountable for implementing them. That's really the essence of entering into this kind of mentor relationship: getting ideas and being held personally accountable for what you know you need to do next.

There's something about the feeling of a good mastermind group that creates very close relationships and very high levels of achievement. For example, I take part in a mastermind group made up of some of the nation's top professional speakers, called a Speakers Roundtable. It's composed of 20 elite and successful speakers in America. (You can learn more about them at SpeakersRoundtable.com.) We get together twice a year in person and also have monthly calls and updates to work on our business and personal initiatives. It's a very tight group and hard to get invited to participate in. Frankly, I'm honored to be part of a group of such thought leaders. Two things that make it work as well as it does is the power of peer pressure and the depth of experience of the members. You really don't want to show up for one of those meetings, or dial in to one of those calls, without having taken the actions that you told the group you were going to take!

I'm also part of a mastermind group organized through EO, the Entrepreneurs Organization (eonetwork.org). This particular group gets together once a month in what's called an E.O. forum session, where 6 to 12 of us go over business and personal issues. It's noncompetitive, confidential, and very tight. The confidentiality and the rapport are necessary because entrepreneurs often don't get the opportunity for unbiased feedback from the people they work with. If they run the company, they can't confide in their employees, and bringing problems up with their spouses or other family members usually creates conflict or varied advice. So this group is an invaluable tool and one of the big reasons I really believe in the concept of mastermind. When these groups are put together properly, they can be extremely powerful.

What you have to avoid, though, is a group that is competitive, where people are trying to show each other up or score points on each other. In those cases, people are hesitant to talk about what they do because they are afraid their competition will capitalize on a unique idea they come up with. These groups can fail when they're not made up of prosperity-minded individuals who are truly interested in hearing constructive criticism and letting the group serve as a collective accountability master. When egos get in the way and judging happens, the group falls apart. You also need to watch out for cases when one person starts to dominate the group, either with their own rules or their own needs.

The key for success is to have a mastermind group that's not too big and not too small—between 3 and 10 is a good target—and is made up of diverse individuals who are all critical thinkers interested in getting good feedback. I mean feedback that will help them grow, personally and professionally. Members must be givers, not takers, and must respect each other's confidentiality.

One more thing: To enjoy the benefits of having an accountability master within one of these groups, you have to be willing to be somebody else's accountability master. You have to be sincerely interested in the success of the other person. You have to be a giver, not just a taker.

MENTOR GROUP THREE: LEGACY MASTERS

This is what happens when you choose to study and model the best practices of mentors you don't know personally. Once you have decided on your role, and you know exactly what it is you want to achieve, you find people who have done it already, you ignore the fact that you don't know them, and you learn as much as you can, so you can model their example.

Our technology and the Internet make it possible to learn from mentors using not only traditional sources like books or CDs, but also social media and YouTube. So no, you may not necessarily know your mentor on a personal level, but thanks to these new resources, you can get direct instruction from them and learn an amazing amount about what they've done in their lives. That means you can learn new skills, master new lessons, adapt new ideas—and these can all help you improve. For example, if I wanted to model my leadership approach very closely after Steve Jobs, using his life lessons and experiences, it's now possible for me to do that. This kind of mentor is key to unlocking our superpower.

In my own life, everything I've ever accomplished has been based on legacy mentorship magic. When I was in a detention center as a young kid, someone gave me a cassette program of *The Psychology of Winning* by Dr. Denis Waitley. (For those of you too young to remember, cassettes played audio programs, what today would be an MP3.) Those cassettes changed the course of my life. That was the first time I had ever heard positive programming, like "If you think that you can do it, you can; stop letting your past become an anchor that holds you back." That audio program was the start of a long journey of personal and professional growth and development.

Soon after hearing that program, I started my first business. I let go of the past and started using the lessons I had gotten from that mentor, whom, of course, I had never met, never worked with, and never knew. Years later, I finally got to meet Dr. Waitley at a conference where we were both speaking, and I got to share with him just how much his earlier work had meant to me.

You need these types of people in your life, these great figures. They are the people who have scaled the heights and reached the top of the mountain. You need to learn what path they followed . . . so you can follow it yourself.

There is power in the right relationships, and having a mentor for personal or professional growth can be a vital asset in achieving your goals. Studies show that we are as successful as the people in our social circles. Who are the people you surround yourself with? Are they successful people? Do they have a positive, can-do attitude? Have they achieved things in life that you are striving for, and perhaps have insights that could help you along the way? Or are your closest friends always complaining, down on their luck, seeming to fail at everything they do? The people you hang out with can make a huge difference in your ability to achieve success.

Why stay stuck in a rut or reinvent the wheel? Study successful people. Discover what makes them tick. What are their thought processes? How positive is their attitude about life? Find people you would like to emulate, be like, be a friend, and ask if they would be willing to be your mentor. Leverage your time, and spend time with positive, healthy, happy people who are on the ball and know how to use their superpowers to get things done. Emulate your mentors; show them that the valuable time they shared with you has not been wasted. Show them that you've used the tips and tools they have shared with you to achieve your own success.

Harness the power of the mastermind group—right now!

You now know about the importance of finding a mentor. I also encourage you to find or start a mastermind group just as soon as you possibly can. It might meet once a week, twice a month, or even once a month. You might meet for coffee at Starbucks, on a conference call, a GoToMeeting, or a video chat.

Select a small number of people you feel will work well together and initiate your mastermind group. Several of my friends and business colleagues actively participate in multiple groups—each helps them target different areas of their personal and professional goals for continuous improvements.

ACTION STEP: CREATING A MASTERMIND GROUP

If you're on the search for a mentoring relationship, in your perfect world, who would you like to spend time with who could help you move farther, faster along your path? (Consider including "legacy" mentors like Steve Jobs or Napoleon Hill on this list.)

1.

2.

3.

4.

5.

Who would you like to mastermind with?

1.

2.

3.

4.

5.

Mentoring is a brain to pick, an ear to listen, and a push in the right direction.

—*John Crosby*

We make a living by what we get, we make a life by what we give.

—*Winston Churchill*

Be the change you want to see in the world.

—*Gandhi*

In every art beginners must start with models of those who have practiced the same art before them. And it is not only a matter of looking at the drawings, paintings, musical compositions, and poems that have been and are being created; it is a matter of being drawn into the individual work of art, of realizing that it has been made by a real human being, and trying to discover the secret of its creation.

—*Ruth Whitman*

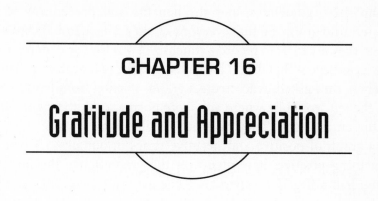

CHAPTER 16

Gratitude and Appreciation

We're still discussing leverage, and we've just talked about using mentoring as a superpower. I feel it's important to discuss the benefits of gratitude and appreciation next, whether that means telling your mentors how much you appreciate their time and insights or thanking your team for helping you get things done. The world moves along more efficiently when you show people a little love and appreciation.

Once you've unleashed and developed superpowers, you'll find ways to benefit from virtually any situation, even a difficult situation...and you'll find you have a sense of gratitude and appreciation for whatever has come your way.

Harnessing gratitude and appreciation can be a difficult skill, but it is essential to your emotional survival. Without denying whatever just happened to you, whether it seems positive or negative at the time, you have to find some way to process it emotionally, learn from it, and, once you've mastered the lesson and come out on the other side, be genuinely *grateful* that it happened to you. That takes a little practice. But you can't be a true superhero without it.

Let me give you an example. When I joined EO, the Entrepreneurs' Organization (eonetwork.org), I went through an orientation to become part of the EO Forum. People talked to us about forum group rules, guidelines, and the benefits and procedures of the mastermind group. So that everyone could get acquainted with each other, they asked us to record a timeline of our lives and identify any significant event that might have changed the course of our lives.

Then, they asked us to create a graph, starting from left to right. On the left would be where you were born and on the right would be the current day. They asked us to plot out events of our lives on a graph of positive and negative times in our lives. If you did something positive, it went up on the graph above the line, but if you had a negative experience, like getting cancer, for example, or something else traumatic occurred, then you plotted below the neutral line. In other words, they tried to get a lifeline experience snapshot of the members of the group.

As we went around the table, my turn to share finally came, and I held up my sheet. My line was straight in a gradual positive progression. The leader of the group told me maybe I didn't understand the exercise, but my response was simple: I understood the exercise. I was appreciative and grateful for everything that had happened to me in my life.

Even though I grew up as a troubled teenager in foster care and detention centers, I was grateful for those experiences. I was a punk kid who carried a 9mm handgun, a terrible school student, and just a generally reckless kid. I was adopted and I spent a lot of time running around on the streets. Now I don't want to give you the wrong impression—I never missed a meal or shot anybody—but I was certainly a misguided youth. But I've found that now, looking back, those weren't actually negative times in my life *because I was learning all the time*. I was learning what I wanted and what I didn't want in my future.

So instead of labeling a specific moment in my life as positive or negative, I've been able to turn the perspective of the negative things in my life into something positive . . . because I believe that life is a gift and hold appreciation and gratitude in my heart.

TAKE A STEP BACK

If you're allowing your fears and resentments about your past, your relationships, your career, or any other part of your life to hold you back, you need to take a step back. *Evaluate what there is to be grateful about in that situation.* What do you appreciate about that situation? Maybe what you can appreciate about that situation is a bad situation, and you now need to get out of it. And you need to do something different. That's what they call a great leap forward. Make the choice; it's your life. That's something to be grateful for.

Now, I'm aware that some people may be coming to this book from the perspective of having been through major traumatic experiences in their past, like abuse, physical injury, or war. My message to you is that I am not a therapist: If you've got something that's dominating your life and taking you to a negative place on a regular basis, you need to look at what you have to do to change that. However, let me also point out that, once you've processed whatever it was that happened to you, you are still alive. You are above ground. And that is definitely something you can choose to be grateful for.

There are a lot of people out there who are dead at the age of 25. They just don't get buried until they're 65 or older. They've given up on their talents, goals, and dreams. Years ago, I was invited to train at the Olympic Training Center in Colorado Springs, Colorado. It was a speed skating camp for athletes who qualified. I was able to train there in 1984 and 1987, and while I didn't make the team, it was a fantastic experience. I could have easily just closed the book right there and said, "Well, I didn't make it. My life's over." But I didn't. You can't let one event close out your life early and become your entire entity. You are much more than a job title or role in your life. You are multifaceted and have many different roles. You can't let these events prevent you from seeing the world clearly. If something traumatic happened in your life, you can draw whatever lessons from that experience to support you. Eventually, it's your choice.

It really is a mind-set, and that is what this book is about. Allow yourself to use your superpower to transform what you think about what happened to your life, and see what you can do to have appreciation and gratitude related to the experience.

Remember the story I shared earlier about the employee who embezzled funds and stole inventory? He was in charge of my accounting, and he worked on some special projects for me. I found out that while I was out of town, he illegally entered my building; stole over $20,000 worth of inventory; got online and took all of our passwords to all of our servers; opened up a bank account, a shopping cart account, and a server hosting account; and attempted to open up a competing business using our resources!

Now, you might think that it would be hard to find something to be grateful for in that situation. And you know what? You would be right. When I found out what had happened, I wasn't grateful at all. I was furious, and the incident led to a few sleepless nights. That's called being a human being.

The situation only seemed to get worse. This guy tried to take away one of my largest accounts by convincing them that they could save money by going to him directly and paying a lower commission rate. Yes, I am human. I got even angrier.

Obviously, this could be categorized as a negative event. It was impacting my business to the tune of $175,000. I had to decide what to do. I decided to get past the anger, which I did, and then deal with the situation in a logical, positive manner. So I filed a legal and civil court case after deciding that it was worth the investment of time and mental energy. The key is that I set mental, emotional, and financial boundaries and expectations ahead of time to protect my mental psyche.

Here's the point: I'm not at day one anymore, which means I'm not investing my time and energy and life force in responsive anger and a defense mode anymore. I'm actually glad that this happened.

Read that part again. *I am actually glad that this happened.*

Why? Because it made me realize how loose the accountability was in this person's position. I allowed this to happen by not putting the checks and balances in place to prevent it. That was another life lesson. This guy didn't realize it, but he was doing some important consulting work for my company. He taught me a lot about how to make sure this kind of thing never, ever happens again.

He also gave me a great self-management lesson that I can share (and have shared) with many other people. One of the big reasons I'm writing this book is to help organizations make the most of the people they have: to keep their top employees, to get them to perform at higher levels without them quitting to work somewhere else. But when your organization hits bumps in the road, like mine did, that shouldn't take down your whole company. It's just not something that's worth losing your company, or your own emotional balance, over. You process it. You decide what happens next. Take corrective action. And then you move on.

Everyone gets life lesson tests . . . and you will keep getting these types of tests until you pass them. If you're really serious about having a positive attitude, then when something like what happened to me happens to you, you won't spend weeks or days or months or years cursing at the person or the event. If that's your reaction, maybe your positive attitude isn't screwed on as tightly as it could be. I don't believe in ignoring a problem and acting like it didn't happen. I believe in working through the problem and moving on. Don't make it harder than it is or easier than it is; just see it for what it is.

Gratitude and appreciation are really about not holding on to a problem once you've dealt with it emotionally and decided what to do about it. Take action . . . and be grateful for the lesson!

The Pilgrims made seven times more graves than huts. No Americans have been more impoverished than these who, nevertheless, set aside a day of thanksgiving.

—*H. U. Westermayer*

When we were children we were grateful to those who filled our stockings at Christmas time. Why are we not grateful to God for filling our stockings with legs?

—*G. K. Chesterton*

The only people with whom you should try to get even are those who have helped you.

—*John E. Southard*

Gratitude is an art of painting an adversity into a lovely picture.

—*Kak Sri*

Gratitude and appreciation are two more superpowers in your arsenal of tools to efficiently and effectively get things accomplished.

Who in your life are you most grateful for?

1.

2.

3.

4.

5.

Write these names in your Superhero Guidebook.

What experiences in your life are you grateful for?

Write them in your Superhero Guidebook.

Who needs to be on your weekly list of people that you want to show appreciation to for being in your life? List the names here and in your Superhero Guidebook, and describe how you are going to show them appreciation.

1.

2.

3.

4.

5.

I'm sure you have more and other ways to express appreciation and gratitude. Capture your ideas and thoughts in your Superhero Guidebook.

PART 5

Measuring Your Success

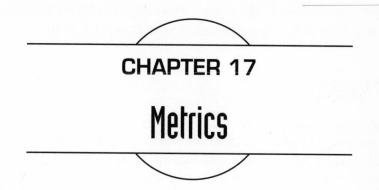

CHAPTER 17

Metrics

So you've got a massive momentum action plan in place, and you're moving things forward to achieve your goals. How are you going to know your plan is working? Unfortunately, society has conditioned many of us to want instant gratification, and while success can come quickly, it rarely happens overnight! Anyone who achieves success has probably spent many years developing the necessary skills and opportunities to reach their goals. The people I admire most were all big failures before they became successes. They failed many times, learned from their mistakes, and picked themselves up and started again, with more experience and insight. Check it out: What do Henry Ford, Walt Disney, and George Foreman have in common? They all went bankrupt before they hit their stride in business!

When you were a child and wanted to learn how to ride a bike, did you roll smoothly down the street the first time you tried? Probably not. You may have started with a tricycle and worked your way up to a real bike with training wheels; then your folks took the training wheels off, and you had to learn a few new skills to be able to balance your bike and ride it really well. Did this process take minutes, hours, days, weeks, or months? Your parents were able to gauge when you were ready for the next step and helped you progress in the skill of riding your bicycle.

To achieve the goals you've set out to accomplish with your massive momentum action plan, you've got to also establish some metrics to be able to gauge whether your plan is working.

THE FLAGPOLE

Once upon a time, there were two guys whose boss told them to measure how tall a certain flagpole was . . . but they didn't know how to go about it. The first guy shinnied up the flagpole, but once he got to the top, he realized that his measuring tape was too short. So he carefully shinnied back down again. His buddy told him that they should ignore the boss's instructions and find something shorter than a flagpole to measure, since their measuring tape was good for only 10 feet.

That didn't seem right, though. Eventually a third guy showed up, saw them debating what to do next, and realized how much difficulty they were having. "Listen, guys," he said. "I'm going to make this a little easier for you." So he took a shovel and started to dig up the flagpole. He dug away, and after about half an hour, he finally got the thing out of the ground and laid it down flat for them. Then he left.

"I don't think that guy was thinking straight," the first fellow said, scratching his head and staring at the flagpole on the ground. "We're supposed to measure how *long* it is, not how *wide*." The boss happened to be standing nearby. When he heard that remark, he fired them both on the spot.

The moral: If you don't measure the right stuff, you're not going to be successful.

ARE YOU MAKING PROGRESS? HOW DO YOU KNOW?

Metrics is a fancy word that means "something, usually a number, that you use to measure your progress toward a goal." Mastering the strategies and tactics outlined in this book is something that all successful people, teams, and organizations learn to do. They get very specific—week by week, day by day, moment by moment—about how close they are to attaining what they want.

Finding the right way to measure your progress and then actually measuring it on a consistent basis is an essential part of the formula for personal success. To master that formula, you have to begin by understanding two critical points:

- First, if you can't measure it, you can't manage it. (That's true whether you're managing yourself or other people. Management is an ongoing task, and learning how to be an effective manager is a superpower. But since we buried the words "I can't," let's change this sentence to "I can master what I can manage." Keeping a close eye on the action is being taken helps you become the master of your universe.)
- And second, only the stuff that gets measured gets rewarded. (Ditto.)

It's not enough to have a clear vision of what success looks like. You also have to have clear *performance indicators* that tell you whether you're getting closer to or farther away from your goal.

KEY PERFORMANCE INDICATORS

In business situations, the term *key performance indicators* (KPI) represents the quantifiable measurements, agreed to beforehand, that reflect the critical success factors of an organization. They differ depending on the organization. For personal use, you can identify what factors you're going to measure, how and when, and add them to your MMAP.

Taking action on your massive momentum action plan without identifying the most important performance indicators that you're going to measure is a little like pointing yourself in a certain direction and then driving across country blindfolded. You may start out with all kinds of confidence that you're headed west, from New York to San Francisco . . . but if you don't find a way to keep your eyes open along the way, watch the road signs, check your gauges, and track your progress toward your goal, you're not likely to make it to your destination.

Performance indicators are analogous to the road signs along the way that allow you to figure out how many miles you've traveled and in which direction. They tell you whether you're on or off track, actually getting closer to San Francisco as you drive (as opposed to, say, New Orleans), and they give you some sense of when you can expect to arrive. There's a reason you don't just get in the car, put a sack over your head, and start driving in what feels like a westerly direction! There has to be something that you observe and measure along the way, something you use to evaluate whether the activity you're engaged in is really working.

How you define *working*, specifically, is up to you. *Working* could mean that whatever you're doing is getting you closer to earning a half million dollars in personal income in the next calendar year. Or it could mean you're closer to losing 30 pounds. It could mean you're closer to delivering a product with zero defects or to winning a 10 out of 10 rating in terms of customer satisfaction from your clients. But whatever it is, you have to be able to confirm that the activity you've chosen to invest time, energy, effort, and attention in is actually delivering the outcome you want. You have to know whether you're making *measurable progress* on what's most important to you and/or your team. I'm sorry to dumb this down for you, but I want you to eliminate any excuses you have for achieving your full potential.

Without key performance indicators to monitor, you could easily be wasting your time and energy. So, what are the key performance indicators you're going to keep track of? What activity can you count and record over time that correlates strongly with the attainment of *your* goal? Don't be scared of that word *correlate*. All it means is that whenever you do something small, over time, you naturally move closer to delivering a bigger result—the result you want.

For example, if you're a salesperson and your goal is to earn a half million dollars in income this year, your performance on that goal might be connected to the number of times you're able to set up an appointment with a qualified new prospect. That'll have a strong correlation with your ability to generate the income you want.

On the personal side, if it's a weight loss goal you're pursuing, one KPI you and your physician might come up with is a measure of how much time you spend exercising and the results of that exercise activity. (For instance: Did your heart rate go up? By how much? For how long?) You want to know the activities you did and then the results of those activities.

I own a Garmin 310XT GPS training watch. It's a cool gadget that tracks multiple exercise activities, records the route with a multitude of measurements, and tracks my heart rate, calories, and exercise times. When I'm done exercising, I can upload the data to Garmin's training website and replay the route, along with analyzing my performance. Over time, I've seen my performance on repeated routes go up and my average heart rate go down, showing me that I'm getting stronger, with more endurance.

In the business sector, the metrics are your financial statements, your income statement, balance sheet, sales reports, conversion percentages, ratios, and the like. If you're in management, you might monitor the number of hours spent on a project and the productivity of those hours. If it's manufacturing, you might look at cycle time, which is the total time required to get from the beginning to the end of the process, as defined by the manufacturer and the customer. (Cycle time includes both process time and delay time.) A business that operates without KPIs is like driving your car on the freeway with all of the windows painted black and no gauges. You are certain to crash and burn.

The point is that you have to know what your metrics are in advance. What does success look like? There's no excuse for not knowing. If you don't know, you need to find out. And even if you do know (or think you do), you need to keep monitoring, testing, and making adjustments to improve your performance.

Selling is the classic example of how important metrics can be and how direct and powerful the connections are between activity and end result. Once you make those connections, you have a process you can follow. For great salespeople, it's all about following the process and understanding your own numbers. All you really need to know is how many sales calls you made and, out of those calls, how many relationships you built and what appointments you set. Out of those appointments, how many qualified leads did you get? Out of those qualified leads, which ones went through the first step of the introduction? You keep it up over time, you take those successive steps along the way, and eventually you find the metrics become part of your routine.

An acre of performance is worth a whole world of promise.
— *William Dean Howells*

Don't rate potential over performance.
— *Jim Fassel*

If you can't describe what you are doing as a process, you don't know what you are doing.
— *W. Edwards Deming*

In God we trust, all others bring data.
— *W. Edwards Deming*

What are you measuring?

What is your most important Key Performance Indicator?

What adjustments do you want to make to improve your performance?

CHAPTER 18

Management

Who is running the store? Who is in charge of reaching your goals? Management doesn't necessarily mean doing the work. But it does mean keeping an eye on what's happening, helping as needed, giving guidance and insights, and keeping people on task to get results. That means daily accountability, weekly accountability, monthly accountability, and annual accountability.

One mistake a lot of managers make is that they think they are looking at a KPI when in fact they're looking at a target. So, for instance, if I'm a manager of a sales team and the only thing I measure is whether a sale closes — if the only question I ask is "Did we get the deal done or didn't we?" — then I am ignoring every other potential metric before that closed deal. That's too bad, because those earlier metrics can help my team affect their outcomes. You can't really change the outcome by the time the end result is in your hand!

Of course, some people like to talk a lot about improving a team's closing skills, but the reality is that success in sales is much more likely to correlate with other activities that come long before the close. My point is that it's not just like that in the world of sales. It's like that just about everywhere.

A more effective manager won't wait until the sales team is hurtling toward the end of the quarter to tell them what they already know: They need to reach the finish line on time.

I like to tell managers something I learned from my friend Dan Burrus, author of *Flash Foresight:* Sometimes the problem isn't the problem. Here's what I mean by that. If I have water all over my floor and I wipe it up, I can talk myself into thinking I'm solving the problem, but in reality, 's the cracks in the wall that allow the water to leak in are the real problem. The key performance indicators have to be set at specific stages so that you really can evaluate what's causing (or preventing) forward progress. This has a relationship to your team's effort, to your tracking of that effort, and then to whether the effort is paying off.

Of course, you may decide—for cash flow reasons, say—that it's important to you to know how much business your salespeople close every day. You may choose to look at that figure closely, and you may even assess daily how much closed business has actually come through compared to how much you expected...but if you don't like the number you see, then guess what? *The problem is not the problem.* You weren't monitoring the right number. You were looking at the outcome, not at what made it possible. What you want is information about whether the process worked so you can intervene and adjust the course if you have to. That means you have to identify something else the team is doing to keep track of.

Finding the right KPI by which to manage your team is likely to be an ongoing challenge, even for an experienced manager. A lot depends on the individual goals of the team members who report to you, their level of career maturity, and the goals you and the team are responsible for reaching. It's really a balancing act. If the KPI is too complicated, people won't pay attention to it, but if it's not detailed enough, you're not going to get enough data to know whether your process is really working.

Here's a list of some commonly used KPIs for teams with sales responsibility:

- Total number of prospecting calls made in a given period.
- Total number of initial appointments set in a given period.
- Amount of face time spent with prospects in a given period.

- Amount of face time spent with customers in a given period.
- Percentage of income from returning customers in a given period.
- Customer attrition rate in a given period. (Obviously, the lower it is, the more effective your sales and service process.)

Or take the example of someone's website. You should manage that with the right metrics, too. The owner of the website may say, "Well, I really don't know what my website is doing!" or "My website's doing great!" But unless they actually look at the website analytics and know how many first-time and repeat visitors there were, how many pages they visited, how many minutes they spent on the website, and the conversion percentages from specific action steps, then they really don't know much of anything. What did your website visitors *do*? Did they sign up, opt in, download something, request more information, complete a form, or buy something? Measuring your success and defining what success looks like is the first step. Then, you want to put in the milestones and the benchmarks so that you can measure your success and make corrective course changes.

> It is an immutable law in business that words are words, explanations are explanations, promises are promises but only performance is reality.
>
> —*Harold S. Geneen*

> Measurement is the first step that leads to control and eventually to improvement. If you can't measure something, you can't understand it. If you can't understand it, you can't control it. If you can't control it, you can't improve it.
>
> —*H. James Harrington*

> The only man I know who behaves sensibly is my tailor; he takes my measurements anew each time he sees me. The rest go on with their old measurements and expect me to fit them.
>
> —*George Bernard Shaw*

What gets measured gets done, what gets measured and fed back gets done well, what gets rewarded gets repeated.

—*John E. Jones*

When dealing with numerical data, approximately right is better than precisely wrong.

—*Carl G. Thor*

Without a standard there is no logical basis for making a decision or taking action.

—*Joseph M. Juran*

You get what you measure. Measure the wrong thing and you get the wrong behaviors.

—*John H. Lingle*

What are you and your team accountable for on a daily basis?

On a weekly basis?

On a monthly basis?

On a quarterly basis?

On an annual basis?

PART 6

Course Corrections

CHAPTER 19

Innovation Insights

There's a great story I've heard about the Apollo space flights from the 1960s. Apparently, during one of their trips to the moon, the astronauts were off course 98 percent of the time. Fortunately, they went through multiple course corrections and had good enough feedback systems to actually hit the target of landing on the moon. And by the way, they did that with far, far less technology than you have in your iPhone. Actually, they did it with less computing power than is needed now to run a greeting card that plays a song when you open it.

Or consider the example of a plane flying from New York to Los Angeles: If it's off by only half of a percent, that translates to being 600 miles off course from the destination. You need measurements to make sure that you're on track, and you need the feedback loop set up to get you the information that ensures your success. Very often, the right course correction requires something I refer to as innovation insight.

Innovation insight means finding brand-new ways of accomplishing the task you have set out for yourself. In other words, maybe the old tried-and-true ways may not work for you. Maybe you need to be a little more creative and innovative about what success looks like and how you're going to get there. For example, if I say I want to lose 25 pounds and I want to run three miles a day, eat only 1,200 calories, and join the YMCA, those are all tasks and to-dos. But if I want to get more creative, I might also say, "I'm going to park farther away from the building every day. I'll make sure that I walk after lunch." That way, I'm expanding the lens outside the typical strategies . . . and looking for ways I can get new results doing things in a different way.

Modeling the success strategies of other people can be one way to do this. You could start looking at what other people do in other industries or other types of businesses and then adapting them to your own business or career.

Being innovative means expanding the lens and listening closely to your own self-talk, so you can catch yourself when you're tempted to say or think, "I can't." Whenever you are tempted to talk yourself into that limiting belief, remember that someone, somewhere, is thinking, "I can" and is doing it right now.

Innovation means being a little restless with standard operating procedures. It means finding creative new ways to accomplish the tasks that are most important to you. There have been so many innovative people throughout history that you can use as role models: Edison, Ford, Disney, and the Wright Brothers have all become icons as a result of their relentless drive to innovate, and in our own time, Steve Jobs has, too. These people were not bound by the status quo, and you don't have to be, either.

Henry Ford used to say, "If I had asked people what they wanted, they would have said 'faster horses'!"

Ford and those other brilliant innovators believed that there was a better way, even if it wasn't obvious at the moment. People thought they were crazy, but they persistently kept looking for newer, better ways to make something happen until those crazy dreams ultimately became a reality. Every time you turn on a light (Edison), drive down a highway (Ford), go to Disney World (Disney), take a flight in an airplane (the Wrights), or listen to a song you've downloaded on iTunes (Jobs), you're proving the power of restless innovation.

Even though you may already have a solid plan in place, may already be effectively managing your projects, and may be checking metrics to be sure what you are doing is working, I encourage you to keep an open mind about innovation.

Innovation is a superpower! And no, you don't have to be the one to come up with the next great innovative idea that will transform everything. You just have to be open to the thought that there might be a better way, and if your mentor or a person on your team has a suggestion, be open to it, evaluate it, and then make an informed and educated decision on implementing this new innovative thought to speed up the process of reaching your goals.

> If you're not failing every now and again, it's a sign that you're not doing anything very innovative.
>
> — *Woody Allen*

> The most successful people are those who are good at Plan B.
>
> — *James Yorke*

> Daring ideas are like chessmen moved forward; they may be beaten, but they may start a winning game.
>
> — *Goethe*

Use your superpowers. Be creative. Be innovative. Look at the situation differently from a variety of perspectives. Find something new that you can do, something you've never tried, but that looks like it has a shot at getting you closer to what you want. Try it . . . and then measure the results carefully to find out whether it actually works better. If it doesn't, stick with what you're doing or try something else. But if it does, then hold on to it with both hands!

CHAPTER 20

Test, Track, Modify, Repeat

If you have established a goal for yourself and you've been taking consistent and massive action, but you find you are not getting the results you want, you should know that continuing to do what you're doing is most likely *not* going to get you where you want to go. In fact, it is proof that you may be crazy. My source on this is Albert Einstein, who said that "continuing to do the same thing over and over again and expecting a different result is the definition of insanity"!

So the question for any true superhero is: Are you willing to course-correct? Are you willing to notice whether you are getting closer to what you want and make minor or major shifts in the actions you are taking to achieve your goals? And here's a question that's just as critical: Are these adjustments course corrections consciously designed to keep you on course or distractions that move you further away from reaching your goals?

For a marketing specialist, one of the key things in analyzing whether an advertisement or campaign is working is to use the following formula: test, track, modify, repeat. It's a great tool for advertising, and it's a great tool for life, too.

Here's how it works online. You first establish a baseline, or control, and then you perform a test. This could be an A/B split test of two website landing pages with different headlines, so you can track which version of the website page (also known as a *landing page*) performs the best. Once you've identified which page pulls the best result, that becomes your new A page (or control page) that you measure against. Then you modify one element on page B and repeat the A/B split test again. If you pay attention and control the variables, you can know for sure—not just have a feeling, but have absolute certainty—about which works better, A or B.

As I say, while this approach holds true for making corrections to increase marketing performance, it's also a solid framework to use for making course corrections for any goal or objective in life. You test, and then you track your performance over time, modify your course, and continue on your journey.

So how does that simple principle apply to a personal goal? Let's use me as an example: I'm a type-A personality. I've been self-employed almost my entire life. I control my own environment; I follow the rules, but I'm also open to changing them. I'm very opinionated, but I believe that I can learn from everybody else.

Now, my management style in the early years of my business operations was strictly command and control—if someone didn't do something the way I wanted it done, I was the first person to bitch at them and say, "Hey, what the hell? This isn't right. We've got to fix this." When I didn't like something, I came on too strong.

Well, using that poor leadership and management approach, I lost a few good employees, and the ones who stayed weren't always all that happy.

In fact, I realized that I was driving away people who were probably trying to help me but decided I wasn't open to their help. I realized that no matter how bad the problem I was complaining about might be, I was always at the scene of the crime. I decided it was time to make a course correction. I read some books, went to some leadership and management seminars, and learned several tactics and tools for improving my management style.

I started testing different strategies to determine what would work better than what I was doing by default. I started testing new A and B pages to see which approach would deliver the best result for me. And guess what? I ended up loosening the reins a little. I started testing the leadership training, confirming that it worked, and putting it into action. Here's an example of a B page I tested that eventually became my A page: A couple of years ago, a client called complaining that a bunch of flyers we designed and printed for her event hadn't reached the hotel yet. I checked with my shipping manager to track the shipment and get proof of delivery. I said, "Jim, did you send it 2nd-day air, and did you track the package?" He said, "Sorry, Ford. I thought I sent it out 2nd-day air, but the default shipping method is ground, and it shipped out ground, meaning that it will not get to the hotel in time for the event." He had a very scared look on his face and clearly was concerned about how I was going to react. Why? Well, for one thing, the flyers were not going to get there in time, and now we have a problem. And for another, Jim may have seen me overreact to that kind of thing in the past. Who knows?

This time around, though, I said, "Jim, it's no problem—just call the local FedEx Kinko's and send them a new PDF file so they can print them and get them to the client on time. It'll cost us a little bit of money."

He came back to me and told me that it was going to end up costing $695 to have them printed, and I said, "Well, we've got to take care of the client, so just do it, and next time please double-check your work."

Later, after arranging for the reprinting and delivery of the flyers, Jim came into my office and said, "I just really want to thank you for how you handled that situation. I was really expecting you to be very upset with me and angry." I told him, "You know, mistakes happen, but my question to you is did you learn from it?" He said yes, and I really believe he did.

So again, through the years of the mistakes I've made and continue to make, I've been able to become a little wiser. From a personal standpoint, I'm constantly looking at what my baseline is. What behavior can I test today to see improved results? What B page can I test against my current A page?

CAN SOMETHING ELSE WORK BETTER?

We're talking about keeping an eye out for new ways of doing things and then testing whether they work better than what we're doing right now. Once I had a very cynical employee who took an extremely negative approach to just about everything she did. One day I sat her down and said, "Look, I realize that cynicism is a strategy you use to protect yourself, I understand it, and we don't need to get into it. I don't want to psychoanalyze you or anything. But for the next couple of days I want you to practice smiling. When you go into meetings, instead of having your head down, instead of making snide remarks, just smile . . . and at the end of the week, let's see whether you've gotten better results or better performance. Are you willing to give that a try?"

She was. She changed her strategy. And she found a B page that worked better than her A page. She was able to see the feedback from everybody else she was working with. Now the team's happier, she's happier, her results are better, and she learned a new skill. So how can we be sure that it's the smiling that changed the outcome? Or how can I correct for any other variable that may have caused the change?

This is where we need to be sure to take your strategy to your Superhero Guidebook. You need to document exactly what you're going to do and what you're changing, and you have to keep track of your results. In direct response marketing, you don't want to change more than one element at a time because otherwise you won't know what changed the result.

As a practical matter, when you are planning the new pages you want to test in your life, you're probably going to want to change only one thing at a time and use that change as the strategy you're keeping an eye on. That's what worked for me.

These are all just tools in your toolbox. My outcome with this book is for you to be able to go to your toolbox and have more than a hammer. As we've all heard, if the only tool you have is a hammer, then every problem you run into looks like a nail. What I want to do is have you add more tools to your toolbox so you can use different strategies to deal with different situations.

REACTIVE OR ADAPTIVE?

There are two approaches to life we all have to consider: reactive or adaptive. A reactive strategy is typical of people who are very set in their ways and constantly reacting to situations the same way. An adaptive strategy is one where the person incorporates new feedback, events, and viewpoints. One of the things that I've noticed over the years is that the growth potential of any team or organization is usually determined by the person at the top, not by the rest of the enterprise. If that person at the top is primarily reactive, the growth potential is low. If the leader is primarily adaptive, the growth potential is high.

I was a very reactive person in the earlier part of my life—I interrupted people, I didn't listen very well, and I still struggle with this at times. My operations manager used to say, "Are you listening to me? Or are you just waiting for your turn to talk?" What I've learned is that being reactive was actually a tool for me, and it was able to get me a certain level of success in certain ventures, but not in the long run.

Being adaptive has proved a much better and wiser strategy for me. To be adaptive to the situation—for instance, in dealing with the problem with the flyers that I mentioned—is an important sign of emotional intelligence. It's one of the things I am proudest of achieving in my life. I wasn't adaptive at all in my 20s and 30s. Creative and innovative, yes, but not very adaptive in my attitude or opinions. I'm more adaptive now, and that means the potential of my entire organization is higher. Now, if there is something that I'm upset with, it's when someone comes to me unprepared four or five times in a row, and each time I've told them to do things a certain way. Then, I still get a little frustrated. In that case, they set an expectation and didn't hit it.

The point is that you have to learn to diagnose the situation before you prescribe a solution, and you have to make sure that you're getting all the facts.

Here's an example of what I mean. Recently, I had lunch with Jeffrey Hayzlett, who wrote a new book called *Running the Gauntlet*. Jeffrey is a global business celebrity and former Fortune 100 C-suite executive. He asked me whether I knew a certain PR person who was at the same conference where we were both speaking in Las Vegas. (We'll call the PR guy John.) John was at the conference at the networking event. John had approached Jeffrey by saying, "Hey, I'd like to spend 10 minutes with you and show you some ideas for taking your business to the next level."

The problem was that's the same pitch this guy has thrown at a thousand other speakers who aren't in Jeffrey's league. John had absolutely no idea who he was talking to. Jeffrey already is a TV producer, he already has multiple TV shows, he was on *The Celebrity Apprentice* with Donald Trump, and he is a best-selling author. How the heck is John going to take Jeffrey's business to the next level if he doesn't even know who he's talking to? If you ran into Paul McCartney, didn't recognize him, and told him you were all ready to help him learn how to put together a number-one album, what kind of response do you think you'd get?

John took a completely reactive approach. He pitched Jeffrey before he had asked any questions, before he had any understanding of the person he was dealing with, and even though he had made no effort to fill in any of those blanks, he jumped in completely unprepared and proposed a solution. By doing that, he completely damaged his reputation with this (important!) prospect. Jeffrey now thinks he's an idiot and will never hire him.

Let me repeat: You have to diagnose first, before you jump to conclusions or attempt to offer advice. You need to have course correction. You need to make sure that you're paying attention to what the marketplace says and what the feedback about you is, minute by minute, day by day, year round.

When you keep getting the same feedback from different sources, that's a sign that you need to do some more work in this area. If everyone around you tells you that you're difficult to work with, the problem probably isn't that everyone is out to get you. The problem, in all likelihood, is that you're difficult to work with and need to look at what you can change in your communication. In my case, everyone kept telling me, "Hey, you're not listening; you never let me finish." Now, I have to be fair here: Every once in a while, that's still a problem for me and something that I struggle with. But that reaction is not anything I have to deal with anywhere near as often as I used to. The difference is that now I'm past the delusional mode and I'm into a mode where I'm working on implementing new strategies. I'm asking myself: What do I need to differently here? Do I need to stop and count to 10? Do I need to bring someone else into the conversation? Do I have to pause and find some new resources so that I can learn new skills that will allow me to be better at whatever it is I want to accomplish?

The only way to know if what you're doing works is to *test it!*

The only way to know if you're getting the results you want is to *track it!* (Watch your metrics!)

The way to avoid insanity is to *modify it!* Tweak it, make an adjustment, correction, or change, so that you can expect a different result.

Then *repeat it!* Repeat it with the modifications you've made, and start the whole process all over again.

This process of making course corrections is what allows you to put all your superpowers into action at full strength. So don't skip this part! This is the step that will have to be repeated over and over and over again until you successfully reach your goals. This is the process that every great individual achiever, and every great company, has followed to make breakthroughs, dominate markets, and capture the imagination of consumers.

Goal setting has traditionally been based on past performance. This practice has tended to perpetuate the sins of the past.
                                                              —*Joseph M. Juran*

Experience isn't so important. . . . What is important is ideas. If you have ideas, you have the main asset you need, and there isn't any limit to what you can do with your business and your life.
                                                              —*Harvey Firestone*

There is no one giant step that does it. It's a lot of little steps.
—*Peter A. Cohen*

Great things are done by a series of small things brought together.
—*Vincent van Gogh*

Success is the sum of small efforts, repeated day in and day out.
—*Robert Collier*

Patience and perseverance have a magical effect before which difficulties disappear and obstacles vanish.
—*John Quincy Adams*

Success is going from failure to failure without losing your enthusiasm.
—*Winston Churchill*

That which we persist in doing becomes easier, not that the task itself has become easier, but that our ability to perform it has improved.
—*Ralph Waldo Emerson*

What process are you testing right now?

How are you tracking your results?

What modifications will you make?

When will you repeat the process to see whether or not it works better than what you were doing before?

PART 7

Celebration

CHAPTER 21

Reward Yourself

The last step in the ongoing journey is the simplest, but for some people, it isn't easy.

Are you waiting until you arrive at your final destination to celebrate your success? Do you realize that every small step along the way that is moving you toward your ultimate goal is something to celebrate?

Keep your long-term outcome in mind, but set some benchmarks along the way to give you and your team something to celebrate. Learning to enjoy the ride—and celebrate successes both large and small—can help you live in an attitude of gratitude.

BENEFITS OF ACKNOWLEDGING YOUR SUCCESSES

When you take the time to celebrate, you increase your positive neural pathways in your brain. This helps increase your motivation and helps you develop a positive attitude. It reinforces your desired behaviors and makes it more likely that you'll take massive action toward your goals. To celebrate, you have to take time to reflect back on your accomplishment, and that gives you time to review where you're at, what you got done, and where you want to go. You don't have to wait until you've reached the big goal to celebrate; in fact, I suggest you set up mini celebrations and maxi celebrations. Remember, each small success is another step in the right direction.

CELEBRATE THE SMALL STEPS

While writing this book, I set word counts on my calendar that I wanted to achieve. Next to it, I would put some type of reward. When I got done with the outline and submitted the book to Wiley, I treated myself to a sports massage. And then once I received the book deal, my wife and I celebrated at our favorite restaurant. I don't watch much TV, and when I do, it's from recorded programs on my DVR. The recorded programs usually back up and get deleted before I get a chance to watch them. So I made myself write at least 3,000 to 5,000 words before I took a break to watch a little TV. Now that the manuscript is almost done, I'm going to schedule a few days off and enjoy the downtime. Your celebration doesn't have to be a big deal. It can be something you do by yourself or share with other people. The important part is that it makes you feel good and conditions positive responses for your accomplishment.

Here are a few great ways to celebrate your success:

- Go to a day spa.
- Take a vacation.
- Go shopping.
- Write a blog post.
- Play a musical instrument.
- Take a walk in the park.
- Read a fiction book.
- Connect with your friends on Facebook.
- Take dance lessons.
- Write in your Superhero Guidebook.

- Capture the moment with photos.
- Record and post a video to YouTube.
- Pay to get your house cleaned.
- Buy flowers.
- Go for a run.
- Walk your dog, or get one and then walk it.
- Send thank-you cards to everyone who supported you.
- Tell the media about it.
- Go out to a movie.
- Spend the day with your family.
- Go to a concert or play.
- Attend a sporting event.
- Tweet your accomplishment.
- Listen to the radio.
- Take a nap.
- Give yourself a certificate for a job well done.
- Go out dancing.
- Spend a day in total silence.
- Go to the gym.
- Have a party.

Celebrating your success is much more than just telling other people about it. It's making sure that you recognize your progress on your journey toward your goals. If all you ever do is focus on the negative or the problems in your life and ignore the positive things, then you will certainly kill your dreams and lower your motivation to succeed. If you just focus on the negative and don't reward yourself for the positive, you will chip away at your self-confidence. If you find yourself focusing on only the things you did wrong, stop and ask yourself, "What are at least three things that I did right today?"

TAKE TIME TO SMELL THE ROSES

In the late 1990s, I was presenting seminars for popular public seminar companies. This involved being on the road for three weeks of each month and traveling around the globe to big cities and mostly smaller cities. These public seminar companies targeted the smaller communities because there was less competition in smaller markets. I would fly out on a Sunday night, present on Monday 9 A.M. to 4 P.M., and then drive to the next event city. I would repeat that process each day and fly home on Friday night. I did this for over three years and presented literally hundreds of full-day and multiday programs on a variety of business-related and personal growth topics. My friends thought I had a glamorous life, but I mainly saw airports and hotel meeting rooms. Looking back, I should have taken time to smell the roses and explored more of my surroundings. But I didn't. I presented, packed up, drove to the next hotel, ate room service, and watched a movie in the room, and then I repeated the process. What a shame, because I didn't take the time to really get to know any of the attendees or really appreciate the successes along the way. I certainly didn't celebrate the small steps along the way. My health suffered because I wasn't working out. My home life relationships suffered because I wasn't there. I was pretty much a speaking robot focusing on that one week a month between speaking tours.

Everything is a choice. And I knew that it was time to make some serious choices. My first decision was to celebrate the fact that I knew something needed to change. My second decision was to revisit my roles and goals and what I wanted in my life. I recognized that I needed to be more focused on the moment and celebrate my successes each day. My focus changed from just giving great presentations to really connecting with the audiences to make a lasting impact. I then took the time to pursue other revenue channels, develop more training resources, and raise my speaking rates so that I could present less on the road and earn more money. I resigned from the public seminar companies as a contract trainer and grew my keynote speaking and consulting business. I wrote in my journal more and took more pictures and videos of the people and places around me. Each night before I went to sleep, I celebrated the things I had learned, the people I had communicated with, and my accomplishments. Your celebrations can be big or small—you decide, but make sure you do it.

CHAMPAGNE MOMENTS

My wife is a Pilates instructor who certifies other Pilates teachers. She tells her clients the story of fitness pioneer Joseph Pilates celebrating "champagne moments" with his clients. If there was an exercise they were unable to do, a challenge for daily life activities, or a fitness goal that they were working on, when they achieved it, Joe would actually stop all activity in the studio, pop the cork on a bottle of champagne, and pour it in Dixie cups, and everyone would toast to their success! A celebration of achievement. I'm not suggesting that you drink alcohol as a celebration, but I do want you to give yourself positive rewards on a regular basis. Don't reward negative behavior with a positive result. Reward yourself for making the positive efforts along the way on your journey to fulfillment.

My wife recently published a very cool fitness journal. It's titled *Be FIT Journal*. This handy fitness logbook is designed to help you see a snapshot of your workouts for the next five years. Each page has five rows for recording your workouts, so in year one, you use the top row through the entire book. Then in year two, you go back and start at the beginning and record your second-year workouts on row two, and so on. It's an amazing way to look back at your progress over time. You can get your copy at www.Centerworks.com.

- Exercise and wellness activities will keep you strong, fit, and flexible.
- Discipline and consistency will help you reach your goals.
- Tracking what you do in your *Be FIT Journal* will help keep you accountable.

Develop lifetime wellness habits, and use your *Be FIT Journal* to see your progress and celebrate it from year to year for the action steps you take that help you reach your health and fitness goals.

Share your superpower of appreciation with those around you who are supporting the achievement of your goals. Share a copy of *Superpower!* with someone you care about.

When you started this journey to develop your superpowers, I hope you had a goal for improving one or more areas of your life. I hope this book has given you things to think about, discuss, or even disagree with. Even better, I hope the processes and action steps in this book will transform your results. Let me ask you now:

What are you going to do to celebrate achieving your success?

Just as important, what are the smaller benchmarks along the way that you will be able to celebrate, knowing that you're heading in the right direction to ultimately achieve your goals?

What will you do to celebrate the (significant!) benchmark of completing this book?

Whatever it is, I hope you follow Joe's example—and find a way to build some champagne into the celebration. Here's to your superpower!

List Five Ways to Celebrate Your Successes

1.

2.

3.

4.

5.

Thinking of others? Write them in your Superhero Guidebook.

Celebrate what you want to see more of.

—Thomas J. Peters

Everything is created from moment to moment, always new. Like fireworks, this universe is a celebration and you are the spectator contemplating the eternal Fourth of July of your absolute splendor.

—Francis Lucille

Share our similarities, celebrate our differences.

—M. Scott Peck

Stop worrying about the potholes in the road and celebrate the journey!

—Barbara Hoffman

The more you praise and celebrate your life, the more there is in life to celebrate.

—Oprah Winfrey

I hope you will share your champagne moments with your Superpower friends online at www.SuperPowerBook.com.

About the Author

SUCCESSFUL BUSINESS LEADER

An entrepreneur almost since birth—he tried to sell tickets to his kindergarten class for recess—Ford Saeks is now positioned as one of the nation's "Top Business Growth Strategists." Ford's innovative, sales-producing, profit-generating solutions help people reach success in their new or existing business ventures by making every dollar count.

For over 30 years, Ford Saeks has been actively involved in the successful growth and operation of multiple business ventures in a variety of industries. He built his first business at age 16, reaped the profitable rewards, and was labeled "A True Entrepreneur."

Since then, he successfully founded 10 more companies, received three U.S. patents and multiple trademarks, and developed a nice collection of intellectual property. His patented inventions, books, audios, and video products have sold millions worldwide through retail stores, mail-order catalogs, mass merchants, and electronic retailers. He took risks, used his instincts, made lots of mistakes along the way, and figured out what worked in highly competitive marketplaces.

Today, Ford focuses his time on his company Prime Concepts Group, Inc.—an integrated marketing services company that he founded in 1987—and on keynote speaking presentations to audiences around the globe.

BUSINESS GROWTH AND MARKETING SPECIALIST

Ford's extensive background in the business world provides his clients with a unique advantage. Ford is best known for helping organizations find, attract, and keep their customers by leveraging the Internet, social media marketing, and innovative publicity campaigns.

Thousands of people benefit from his television show, *Profit-Rich Marketing,* and his *Success Strategies* column in business and trade publications, listen to him on numerous radio and television interviews, and benefit from his customized consultations, corporate presentations, public seminars, and training resources. He shares real-life advice as someone who has been there in his own ventures and with his many clients. He is a national board member of the National Speakers Association and donates to a variety of charitable organizations. He is married to Aliesa George and lives in Wichita, Kansas.

PROFESSIONAL KEYNOTE SPEAKER AND AUTHOR

All programs are available in keynote, half-day, and full-day presentations. All are customized for the client's needs and desired outcomes.

Ford's Most Requested Speaking Presentations

Business Growth Acceleration™: Improving Your Find-ability, Unique-ability, and Profitability!

This interactive presentation is designed for you and your teams to attract new clients, wow your current customers, and leverage all of your efforts to produce maximum results ... even on a limited budget.

You'll learn the three strategies that simplify idea generation to grow your business. Secrets that expand your digital footprint to attract customers like a magnet. Methods that help you shorten your sales cycle, improve conversions, and get massive results. The nontechnical approach to get top search-engine rankings that drive targeted traffic to your website. How to communicate a congruent brand through your website and social media, along with traditional media that give you top-of-mind awareness, more sales, and increased profits.

Common Sense Is a Superpower: A Road Map to Better Decision Making and a Better Life!

Do you want more out of your life and your job with less effort and better results? Have you ever felt that there just has to be a better way to get there? If so, you're not alone. Millions of people, just like you, are faced with many challenges in their professional and personal lives on their journey to success. *Superpower!* takes you on a journey where you'll discover seven steps that will help you solve problems faster, make better decisions, and improve your professional and personal life.

Innovative Marketing Mastery™: Creativity in Action to Produce Profitable Results

Whether marketing is just part of your job or the whole enchilada, whether you're selling products or services or fund-raising for a nonprofit or not-for-profit, there are times when you need to come up with creative new ideas to attract attention and stand out above the competition. This program shows you and your audience creative methods you can use to generate tons of new ideas and improve your sales and marketing efforts.

This high-energy how-to session offers you a multitude of creative marketing techniques for subtly—and not so subtly—getting your prospects and customers to buy more products and services.

Social Influence: How to Monetize Social Media Marketing Efforts to Grow Your Business

Everyone wants more traffic to their website, but what they really want is targeted traffic that converts into sales and repeat customers. This isn't just another how-to presentation on social media. Ford cuts through the clutter and hype so you can maximize your efforts. This presentation is perfect for everyone, regardless of your individual role in the process *or* your level of expertise

His clients include franchise companies, entrepreneurs, major corporations, associations, and convention groups that want impactful presentations with implementable action steps.

Contact Ford Saeks at:

Toll-Free United States & Canada: 1-800-946-7804

Telephone: 316-942-1111

Fax: 316-942-5313

Prime Concepts Group Inc.

7570 W. 21st Street N., Suite 1038A

Wichita, KS 67205 USA

www.PrimeConcepts.com Corporate Website
www.ProfitRichResults.com Speaker Website
www.ProfitRichResultsEvent.com Business Growth Summit
www.GetPaidtoSpeak.com Speaker Training Website
www.SuperPowerBook.com *Superpower* Book Website

Social Media Links:

Youtube.com/primeconcepts PCG YouTube Channel
LinkedIn.com/in/primeconcepts Connect with Ford on LinkedIn
Twitter.com/prime_concepts Follow him on Twitter
Facebook.com/profitrichresults Like him on Facebook

Other Titles by Ford Saeks

Profit-Rich Marketing: Proven Strategies to Help You Grow Your Business

The Internet Profit Kit: 101 Ways to Leverage the Internet and Build Your Online Empire

Marketing Magic

Celebrate Marketing

Keyword Secrets: How to Drive Targeted Traffic to Local and National Businesses

Social Influence: How to Connect, Engage and Convert

Information Entrepreneur Intensive: How to Develop, Package and Promote Information Products

Recommended Resources

The Prosperity Series: Manifest Health, Happiness and Wealth in Your Life ...

You are meant to be healthy, happy, and prosperous. Once you recognize and accept this, it is simply a case of learning the principles that abundance is based on. In this insightful series, you will move from lack consciousness to living in the light of true abundance.

- What creates prosperity consciousness
- The universal laws that govern prosperity
- Why you should embrace critical thinking
- The secret to creating a vacuum for good
- What it takes to manifest prosperity on the physical plane
- Why you are supposed to be wealthy

Five-Book Series by Randy Gage:

101 Keys to Your Prosperity

Accept Your Abundance! Why You Are Supposed to Be Wealthy

37 Secrets about Prosperity

Prosperity Mind! How To

Harness the Power of Thought

The 7 Spiritual Laws of Prosperity

You can claim your FREE digital downloads of the Prosperity Series of books at www.primeconcepts.com/superpower/prosperity.

Business Growth Summit Event with Ford Saeks

Get More Customers, **Penetrate** New Markets, **Increase** Targeted Website Traffic, **Monetize** Social Media, and **Accelerate** Your Results

Each day you're faced with new opportunities and the challenges of how you are going to spend your time and money. Whether you're the CEO, an entrepreneur, or the person responsible for increasing results from marketing and sales efforts, you already know that it is becoming increasingly more difficult to find, attract, and keep your customers.

The good news is—there is no need to panic! The sky is not falling ... these economic times have actually created many new opportunities—if you know how to capitalize on them.

Let me ask you this:

- Are you interested in how to effectively reach a larger target market locally, nationally, or globally and create a steady stream of prospects?

- Have you tried sure-fire marketing techniques, only to have them fail miserably—yet you aren't sure why?

- Do you know the three things you *must* do to get more traffic and improve lead conversions with your website and social media marketing?

For the past few decades, I have been the go-to business growth expert for a variety of businesses in a wide range of industries. My clients range from entrepreneurs and small businesses to top Fortune 500 companies. I have a long list of testimonials—and a history of producing results.

I know firsthand the profit-producing secrets on how to create, improve, and implement proven strategies to immediately increase your response rate, boost sales, reduce risk, and give you a competitive edge ... regardless of your products, services, prices, or industries.

Bottom line: I've spent my life living and breathing business growth marketing strategies, spending my own money with everything from traditional marketing methods to Internet and social media networking tactics.

What if there was a unique event where you could learn how to best leverage your time and marketing dollars to create the most profitable results?

What would it do for your business if you were able to work side-by-side with a marketing expert who gave you the exact strategies necessary to increase the response rate of all your marketing efforts? What if you also walked away with a massive action plan that you can implement immediately to make prospecting easier, get more customers, and increase sales?

I'll show you how to create, improve, and implement proven strategies to increase your sales, grow your customer base, and give you a competitive edge in your business.

So while others are floundering to grow, arm yourself with proven strategies guaranteed to produce results, even in an overstimulated, panic-stricken, slow-to-recover economy.

Watch the video now to see if this event is right for you: www.BusinessGrowthSummitEvent.com.

Invite Ford Saeks to present at your next event! www.ProfitRich Results.com or call 316-942-1111.

Index